CHRISTMAS
WITH GORDON

GORDON RAMSAY

WITH EMILY QUAH
PHOTOGRAPHS BY CHRIS TERRY

Quadrille
PUBLISHING

Project director Anne Furniss
Creative director Helen Lewis
Project editor Janet Illsley
Designer Jim Smith
Photographer Chris Terry
Food stylists Annie Nichols and Steve Allen
Props stylists Cynthia Inions
Home economist Emily Quah, assisted by Cathryn Evans
Production Ruth Deary, Vincent Smith

This edition first published in 2015 by Quadrille Publishing Limited
Pentagon House, 52–54 Southwark Street, London SE1 1UN
www.quadrille.co.uk

Quadrille is an imprint of Hardie Grant
www.hardiegrant.com.au

Text © 2010 Gordon Ramsay
Photography © 2010 Chris Terry
Design and layout © 2010 Quadrille Publishing Limited

ISBN 978 184949 702 2

Printed in China

One Potato Two Potato
Managing director Pat Llewellyn
Christmas with Gordon:
Executive producer Ben Adler
Series producer Paul Ratcliffe
Series food producer Sarah Durdin Robertson
Producer Colin Steele

One Potato Two Potato
102 St Pancras Way
London NW1 9ND

ONE POTATO TWO POTATO

Notes

All spoon measures are level unless otherwise stated:
1 tsp = 5ml spoon; 1 tbsp = 15ml spoon.

All herbs are fresh, and all pepper is freshly ground unless otherwise
suggested.

I recommend using free-range eggs. If you are pregnant or in a vulnerable
health group, avoid those recipes that contain raw egg whites or lightly
cooked eggs.

If possible, buy unwaxed citrus fruit if you are using the zest.

My oven timings are for fan-assisted ovens. If you are using a conventional
oven, increase the temperature by 10–15°C (½–1 Gas Mark). Individual
ovens can deviate by as much as 10°C from the setting, either way.
Get to know your oven and use an oven thermometer to check
its accuracy. My cooking times are provided as guidelines,
with a description of colour or texture as appropriate.

CONTENTS

INTRODUCTION

When I began my career as a young chef, I didn't envisage that I would be on TV or writing a book about Christmas cooking, but without fail, as each year draws to a close, I am inundated with queries. I'm often asked for ideas about food to serve at Christmas parties, the secret to a perfect roast turkey, even what to do with the leftovers.

As a chef and food writer, I have certainly cooked my fair share of festive feasts. But rather than give you a weighty tome of every possible Christmas dish, I wanted this book to be a considered collection of mouth-watering recipes that will impress your friends and family. Whether you are hosting a drinks party for friends, cooking for the main event, or just making a dessert, I hope that, at the very least, you will choose to prepare some of my dishes.

For the main festive meal, I've provided five different menu options, each centred on a classic dish with a modern twist: my roast turkey with lemon, parsley and garlic; a new take on beef Wellington; a tempting honey-glazed ham; easy pan-fried sea bass fillets; and an aromatic roast goose with five spice and honey. I've also included a time plan for each menu, encouraging you to do as much as possible well in advance, to avoid last-minute panics on the day. Of course, you may prefer to mix and match courses, or come up with your own special menu – just think about the balance of flavours and textures.

As the festive entertaining starts on Christmas Eve – or even earlier – and extends right through to New Year's Day, I've included scrumptious dishes that you can easily put together to feed guests at any time, plus ideas for turning cooked turkey and ham, smoked salmon and Stilton into tasty meals and snacks. Some recipes are simple, others more elaborate but rewarding to prepare. Whatever you choose to cook, I sincerely hope you enjoy the festivities with family and friends. Happy Christmas!

CHRISTMAS
FRUIT & NUTS

Seasonal fruits and nuts play an important role in setting the scene at Christmas, lending colour and texture to a variety of dishes. Even a simple bowl of clementines can act as a vibrant centrepiece, perhaps with a few pomegranates added.

I use cranberries profusely in their various forms: cranberry juice for breakfast smoothies and cocktails; dried cranberries in salads, mincemeat, muesli, cakes and biscuits; and the fresh berries in sweet and sour sauces.

Like cranberries, I love using pomegranates. Their seeds lift salads, Middle Eastern stews, desserts and drinks. Pomegranate juice is also great for cooking, as it adds a tart element to a dish, and it's very good for making ice creams and sorbets, too. Bottled pomegranate juice is readily available, but the quality is variable. If you'd rather juice your own fruit, halve or quarter the pomegranates, then tap the skin with the back of a spoon to shake the seeds into a bowl (leaving the bitter membrane behind). Blitz the seeds coarsely in a food processor, then strain the juice through a fine sieve.

Chestnuts – in their shells, vacuum-packed, marron glacé and tins of chestnut purée (both sweetened and unsweetened) – are storecupboard essentials at Christmas. Natural partners to Brussels sprouts, chestnuts are also great in creamy soups, stuffings, cakes, muffins and desserts – including the classic Mont Blanc (meringues topped with cream and chestnut purée). Chestnut flour, with its distinctive sweet flavour, is a product I get particularly excited about, though it is quite tricky to source. If you do happen to come across it, buy a bag and make my chestnut muffins (on page 86).

Walnuts are another favourite. I add them to various sweet and savoury dishes – even my turkey gravy (see page 35), to give it a slightly nutty character. They have a notable affinity with chicory and blue cheese, and I'll often add a handful of toasted walnuts to my salads, soups, rice and pasta dishes, and then finish with a drizzle of walnut oil.

I'm also partial to pistachios – using them to add colour and crunch to biscuits and desserts, for example. And, like the Italians, I often feature pine nuts in festive dishes – their sweet nutty flavour is lovely with radicchio and other winter veg, but also in stuffings and, of course, in cookies, cakes and tarts.

CHEESES

A Christmas cheeseboard is a wonderful way to offer your guests something to help themselves to, as they enjoy a glass of wine. Or, if you haven't had time to make a festive pudding, presenting a lovely cheeseboard, followed if you like by some warm mince pies (either home-made or shop-bought), offers you a quick and easy option at the end of the meal.

It need not be an expensive affair. The key is to pick what you and your guests like to eat and spend wisely. Select a few beautiful cheeses rather than cram your board with numerous mass-produced inferior varieties.

For many, Stilton is a must at Christmas time; I also like Stichelton, a similar blue made from unpasteurised cow's milk. Traditionalists will look for a mature West-country Cheddar – there are plenty of flavourful varieties to choose from, so taste a few to find the one you like best before buying. Similarly a perfectly ripe Brie is always popular. A soft goat's cheese, such as Ragstone, Dorstone or Rosary, is another good choice.

I like to offer a few surprises, such as a young Pecorino from Italy. And I'll sometimes introduce a more unusual soft, creamy cheese, such as a French or Swiss Vacherin, which comes wrapped in a spruce box. This cheese can be enjoyed at room temperature or warmed up in its box to serve fondue-style, with breadsticks or small pieces of toast for dipping.

Do ask your cheesemonger if there are any exciting new cheeses to try – you can always buy a small piece if it seems a bit strong and contentious. It is best to buy cheeses as close to Christmas as possible, particularly if you are serving a young cheese which needs to be eaten fresh. To accompany, don't forget to stock up on crackers and breadsticks. Instead of the usual bunch of grapes, I like to put something different on the cheeseboard – a handful of walnuts, dates and dried figs, and a suitable chutney or fruit jelly, for example.

Take the cheeses out of the fridge before you sit down to eat your starter. Loosen the wrappings and place the cheeses on the cheeseboard. (Like red wine, cold suppresses the flavour of a cheese.) When the meal is finished, wrap leftover cheeses in waxed paper (rather than cling film) to prevent them from drying out in the fridge. And if you need ideas for using up that leftover Stilton we all seem to have at Christmas, have a look at my suggestions (on pages 122–3).

WINES
& OTHER FESTIVE DRINKS

Fortunately there is an excellent choice of wines on offer in supermarkets and specialist shops in a range of prices. In general, opt for a white wine that stimulates and appeals to most tastes, rather than something full and demanding. An aromatic white will serve this purpose, so select according to your budget from: Loire Valley whites, such as Sancerre and Pouilly Fumé; New World Sauvignon Blanc and Bordeaux Blanc Sec (both ideal with party food); Australian Riesling; Gavi di Gavi; New World Chenin Blanc or Viognier.

As for red wines, look for a lively young wine with all-round appeal and the fruit to live up to a variety of flavours. Mediterranean reds in particular could feature here: Southern Italian reds like Primitivo, Salice Salentino and Negroamaro; Tuscan reds and Rioja Crianza. Chilean Merlot and Argentinian Malbec are well worth considering and young Bordeaux, such as Côtes de Bourg, Fronsac and Premières Côtes de Bordeaux, can also be attractive bargains.

And don't overlook rosé – an all year drink now – seek out a dryish wine from Languedoc or Provence.

Of the countless other wine-style options, good non-vintage Champagne, such as Pol Roger or Louis Roederer, is traditional, refined and fun all at the same time; it also makes a perfect accompaniment to smoked salmon. Prosecco and good-quality fizz – from the New World, Loire Valley or even England – also work well, especially with party food.

Sherry and port are not necessarily everyone's first choice, but good-quality Fino and Manzanilla can be a revelation and have the guts to match pretty much anything – though they must be fresh and properly chilled. A glass of pleasantly chilled Tawny port, probably a ten-year-old one, makes a fine drink to go with Stilton or on its own as an aperitif.

CHRISTMAS MENU WINE SUGGESTIONS

ROAST TURKEY: White Burgundy or New World Chardonnay; or Châteauneuf-du-Pape or Californian Cabernet Sauvignon if a red is required.

BEEF WELLINGTON: Rioja Reserva; perhaps a Mâcon Villages to serve with the starter.

GLAZED HAM: Pinot Noir from Australia or a red Burgundy; possibly an English Bacchus with the starter.

SEA BASS: A Riesling from Australia; a Pinot Gris from Alsace with the starter if desired.

ROAST GOOSE: Dry/off-dry Riesling from Alsace or Germany; or Rioja Reserva or Gran Reserva, if red is required.

DRY-ROASTED SPICED NUTS

MAKES 250G

250g mixed nuts, such as Brazil nuts, almonds, walnuts, pistachio nuts

pinch of sea salt

1 tbsp groundnut or other neutral-flavoured oil (optional)

½ tsp cayenne pepper

½ tsp sweet paprika

1 rosemary sprig, leaves stripped

1 Heat a large frying pan, add the nuts and toast gently for a few minutes, shaking the pan constantly to ensure they colour evenly. Once they start to release their natural oils, add the salt and toss well. (If you find that the salt isn't sticking to the nuts, add 1 tbsp oil and toss again.)

2 Once the nuts start to colour, add the cayenne, paprika and rosemary. Toss to ensure the nuts are thoroughly coated. Continue to heat, tossing frequently over a medium heat for a few minutes until the nuts and spices are aromatic. Do not leave the pan unattended as the nuts can burn very quickly at this stage.

3 Tip the nuts into a wide bowl, sprinkle with a little more salt and leave to cool completely. Store in an airtight container unless serving immediately.

4 To warm the nuts, either toss them in a frying pan over a medium heat or gently toast them in a preheated oven at 180°C/Gas 4 for about 10 minutes.

These are ideal nibbles to serve with drinks. You can vary the nuts as you like, or even use a pack of unsalted ready-mixed nuts.

MULLED WINE

There's no better way to welcome your friends and family into your home at Christmas than with warming glasses of deliciously aromatic mulled wine. My version infuses the wine with traditional and modern flavours. Pour a bottle of red wine into a large saucepan and place over a gentle heat. Tie 7 cardamom pods, 5 cloves, 2 star anise, 1 halved cinnamon stick and 1 snipped lemongrass stalk in a piece of muslin to form a bag. Add to the saucepan with the pared zest of 1 orange and the segmented orange flesh, 1 tbsp demerara sugar and 2 chopped preserved stem ginger with 2 tbsp syrup from the jar. Heat gently for 4–5 minutes, stirring occasionally to encourage the flavours to infuse; do not allow it to boil. Ladle the mulled wine into cups or glasses. 4–5 SERVINGS

SMOKED SALMON
WITH AVOCADO AND HORSERADISH
MOUSSE ON PUMPERNICKEL

MAKES 28–30

1 ripe medium avocado

1 tbsp creamed horseradish

1 tbsp lemon juice

sea salt and freshly ground black pepper

75ml double cream

4–5 large slices of pumpernickel or rye bread

225g smoked salmon

dill sprigs, to garnish

1 Halve the avocado and remove the stone, then scoop out the flesh into a blender or food processor. Add the creamed horseradish, lemon juice and some seasoning and whiz to a very smooth purée.

2 Whisk the double cream in a bowl until thick and just holding peaks, then fold in the avocado purée. Taste and adjust the seasoning. Cover and chill for at least an hour until firm.

3 To assemble, remove the crusts from the bread and then cut into bite-sized squares. Cut the salmon into strips and drape them neatly over the bread squares.

4 Place a quenelle or neat teaspoonful of chilled avocado and horseradish mousse on each one. (To shape a quenelle, warm a spoon in hot water, shake off the water, then run the spoon along the surface of the mousse to take up a neat oval shape. Slide it off the spoon onto the smoked salmon.)

5 Garnish each canapé with a dill sprig and arrange on a platter to serve.

Dark, thin slices of nutty, pumpernickel bread provide the perfect background for these colourful smoked salmon bites, although fresh rye or soda bread would work equally well. Good-quality smoked salmon is essential here, as it needs to be able to stand up to the gutsy horseradish.

PUMPKIN TARTLETS
WITH SAGE AND THYME

MAKES 8 TARTLETS OR 32 CANAPÉS

Polenta pastry:

175g plain flour

25g polenta

pinch of fine sea salt

100g unsalted butter

2 large egg yolks

1–2 tbsp cold water

1 medium egg white

Filling:

200ml double cream

10–12 sage leaves, snipped

few thyme sprigs, plus extra leaves to
    sprinkle

sea salt and freshly ground black pepper

300g pumpkin purée (see page 99)

2 large eggs, lightly beaten

3–4 tbsp freshly grated Parmesan

1 To make the pastry, put the flour, polenta and salt into a food processor. Cut the butter into cubes, add to the processor and process briefly until the mixture resembles fine breadcrumbs. Add the egg yolks and 1 tbsp water and pulse until the mixture starts to clump together. If it is too dry, add another 1–2 tsp water, until you can press the dough together into a ball. Wrap in cling film and chill for at least 30 minutes.

2 Meanwhile, for the filling, put the cream into a small saucepan and add the snipped sage, thyme sprigs and a pinch of salt. Bring just to a simmer, then remove from the heat and leave to infuse and cool completely.

3 Roll out the pastry thinly on a lightly floured surface and use it to line eight 10cm tartlet tins, trimming off the excess pastry. Brush the insides with egg white, then place on a baking tray and chill for an hour.

4 Preheat the oven to 180°C/Gas 4. Line the tartlet cases with greaseproof paper and baking beans or dried beans and 'bake blind' for 15 minutes. Remove the paper and beans and return to the oven for 5 minutes. Remove from the oven and lower the setting to 170°C/Gas 3.

5 Strain the herb-infused cream through a fine sieve into a bowl, discarding the herbs. Stir in the pumpkin purée and beaten eggs. Season well to taste. Spoon the filling into the pastry cases, then sprinkle a little grated Parmesan and a few thyme leaves on top. Bake for about 20–25 minutes until lightly golden and set.

6 Let the tartlets cool in the tins before unmoulding. Carefully slice each tartlet into quarters and arrange on a platter to serve.

I came up with this recipe in order to use up some leftover pumpkin purée, but you could of course use tinned purée. Rather than making bite-sized mini tartlets, it is easier to make larger tartlets to cut into wedges to serve as canapés. To enjoy them at their best, serve the tartlets soon after baking.

MARINATED BEEF SKEWERS
WITH GARLIC AND ROSEMARY

MAKES 12–15 SKEWERS

500g sirloin steak, trimmed of fat

2 tbsp olive oil, plus extra to drizzle

1 tbsp Dijon mustard

2 rosemary sprigs, leaves only, finely
chopped

2 garlic cloves, peeled and crushed

1 tbsp lemon juice

about 24 rosemary (or wooden) skewers
(see right)

200g baby plum or cherry tomatoes

200g button mushrooms

sea salt and freshly ground black pepper

1 Cut the steak into 2–2.5cm cubes and place them in a shallow dish. Whisk the olive oil, mustard, rosemary, garlic and lemon juice together in a small bowl. Pour over the beef and leave to marinate in a cool place for at least 2 hours, or preferably overnight in the fridge.

2 To prevent the skewers from burning under the grill, soak them in cold water for about 20 minutes before using.

3 When ready to serve, scrape the excess marinade from the beef. Thread the steak cubes, tomatoes and mushrooms alternately onto the rosemary (or wooden) skewers, from the pointed end. Drizzle a little olive oil over the skewers and season with salt and pepper.

4 Heat up a griddle or the grill and cook the skewers for about 5–6 minutes for medium rare, or until done to your liking, turning and basting them frequently with the marinade.

To me, these rosemary beef skewers are perfect for the festive season as the rosemary is reminiscent of spindly pine needles. You will need to gather long woody rosemary sprigs (ideally from the garden), strip off half the leaves from the base ends and then trim the base of each sprig to create a sharp, pointy end.

PAPRIKA CHICKEN
WITH AÏOLI

MAKES ABOUT 24 SHORT SKEWERS

Paprika chicken:

450g boneless, skinless chicken breasts
   or thighs

2 garlic cloves, peeled and crushed

½ tsp dried oregano

⅓ tsp celery salt

1 tsp sweet smoked paprika

2 tsp lemon juice

1 tsp light brown sugar

1 tbsp olive oil, plus extra to drizzle

sea salt and freshly ground black pepper

Aïoli:

2 medium egg yolks

1½ tsp Dijon mustard

2 small garlic cloves, peeled and chopped

pinch of saffron strands

1–2 tbsp lemon juice, to taste

100ml vegetable oil

100ml light olive oil

1 Soak 24 short bamboo skewers in cold water for at least 20 minutes. Cut the chicken into 2.5cm pieces and place in a large bowl. Add the rest of the ingredients, including a good pinch each of salt and pepper, and mix well.

2 Thread the chicken pieces onto the soaked bamboo skewers and place on a plate. Cover and leave to marinate in the fridge for at least 2 hours, preferably overnight.

3 To make the aïoli, blend the egg yolks, mustard, garlic, saffron and 1 tbsp lemon juice together in a food processor. With the motor running, slowly add the oils through the funnel in a steady stream. Season with salt and pepper to taste, adding a little more lemon juice to sharpen the flavour if you like. Transfer to a serving bowl and set aside.

4 When you are ready to serve, heat up a griddle pan or the grill. Lightly drizzle the chicken skewers with a little olive oil and griddle or grill for 6–8 minutes, turning several times, until cooked all the way through. Serve the skewers on a large platter with the aïoli alongside for dipping.

These Spanish-style chicken skewers, served with a lovely unctuous aïoli, are perfect party fare. To save time on the day, marinate the chicken and make the aïoli the day before. Keep any extra aïoli in the fridge to serve with seafood, a fish stew or grilled meats.

STILTON GOUGÈRES

MAKES 80–90

125ml milk

125ml water

80g unsalted butter, diced

125g plain flour

pinch of sea salt

2 large eggs, lightly beaten

75g Stilton, crumbled

1 Pour the milk and water into a medium saucepan and add the butter. Warm over a low heat until the butter has melted. Meanwhile, sift the flour and salt into a bowl.

2 Once the butter has melted, increase the heat and bring to a rolling boil. As soon as the liquid starts to bubble, turn off the heat and tip in the flour and salt all at once. Beat the mixture quickly with a wooden spoon until it forms a paste that comes away from the sides of the pan. Tip into a bowl and leave to cool.

3 Transfer the choux pastry to a food processor, add the eggs and cheese and blend until smooth. (The pastry can be wrapped and chilled at this stage for up to 24 hours.)

4 Preheat the oven to 180°C/Gas 4. Spoon the pastry into a piping bag fitted with a 1cm plain nozzle and pipe walnut-sized mounds onto a non-stick baking sheet. Dab down the tips of each mound with a dampened finger. Bake for 18–20 minutes, or until risen, golden brown and crisp.

5 Let the gougères cool slightly for a few minutes, then serve.

These savoury cheese puffs may look plain, but they are truly scrumptious. They do, however, need to be eaten soon after baking, otherwise they will lose their crispness. However, you can prepare the choux pastry ahead – even pipe the gougères and refrigerate them on the baking sheets for several hours. Bake straight from the fridge, allowing an extra few minutes in the oven.

STUFFED DATES
WITH HONEY AND PISTACHIO MARZIPAN

MAKES ABOUT 30

100g shelled unsalted pistachio nuts

1 tbsp caster sugar

1½–2 tbsp clear runny honey

1½ tsp lemon juice

½ tsp rosewater, or to taste

icing sugar, to dust

28–30 Medjool or Deglet Noor dates

1 Put the pistachios and caster sugar into a food processor and pulse until the mixture resembles coarse breadcrumbs. Do not over-process, otherwise the nuts may release their oils and become greasy. Drizzle in the honey, lemon juice and rosewater and blend until the mixture starts to clump together.

2 Turn the marzipan onto a surface dusted with icing sugar and knead lightly until soft and smooth.

3 Halve the dates lengthways and remove the stones. Take about a teaspoonful of the pistachio marzipan and shape it into a roll slightly shorter than the length of the date you are filling, dusting it with a little icing sugar to prevent the paste from sticking to your hands.

4 Insert the marzipan into the slit and press the date gently to encase the filling. Put the date in a small waxed paper case and repeat to stuff the rest of the dates.

I was inspired to make these after a trip to Dubai, where sweet, luscious dates are a treat. They are fabulous as sweet canapés.

CHRISTMAS STAR FRUIT PUNCH
I always like to offer an interesting non-alcoholic alternative and this Asian-inspired tropical fruit punch, made from cartons of fruit juice, fits the bill. Pour 250ml passion fruit juice, 750ml pineapple juice and 750ml lychee juice into a large jug. Add the leaves from a few mint sprigs, 1 thinly sliced lime and 1 sliced star fruit. Cover and chill until ready to serve. Just before serving, stir in 500ml soda water and plenty of ice cubes. (You can spike the punch with a glug or two of rum if you like.) 6–8 SERVINGS

CHRISTMAS MENUS

ROAST TURKEY MENU

Roast turkey with lemon, parsley and garlic
Turkey gravy with cider and walnuts
Pork, apricot and pistachio stuffing
Caramelised cranberry and apple sauce
Roast potatoes with chilli and turmeric
Brussels sprouts with pancetta and chestnuts

Light steamed pudding with whiskey cream

PLANNING YOUR TIME

WELL IN ADVANCE...
- Order your fresh free-range turkey. (If, instead, you opt for a frozen turkey, a 5–6kg one will need about 3 days to thaw in the fridge.)

THE DAY BEFORE...
- Make the cranberry and apple sauce. Refrigerate.
- Make the herb butter and use to stuff the turkey. Return to the fridge.
- Make the stuffing and wrap in foil, ready for the oven. Refrigerate.
- Make the pudding and steam, then leave to cool.

6–7 HOURS IN ADVANCE...
- Bring the turkey to room temperature.

4½ HOURS AHEAD...
- Put the turkey in the preheated oven. Baste and lay the bacon rashers over the turkey breast after the first 15 minutes. Baste the turkey every 30 minutes.
- Blanch the sprouts and keep them immersed in chilled water.
- Make the whiskey cream and keep chilled.
- Peel the potatoes and immerse in water to prevent browning.

1½ HOURS AHEAD...
- Take the cranberry and apple sauce from the fridge and put into a serving bowl.
- Parboil the potatoes and drain. Toss in seasoning and hot oil.
- Remove the turkey from the oven and leave to rest.
- Put the potatoes and stuffing in the oven to roast.
- Make the gravy and leave in the pan ready to reheat.
- Steam the pudding for 40–45 minutes to reheat.

ABOUT 15 MINUTES AHEAD...
- Warm your plates and serving dishes.
- Finish cooking the sprouts and gravy.
- Warm the cranberry and apple sauce.

JUST BEFORE SERVING...
- Unwrap and slice the stuffing to serve alongside the hot gravy. Plate the roast potatoes.
- Carve the turkey and serve with all the accompaniments.
- Unmould the steamed pudding, glaze with the maple syrup and serve with the whiskey cream.

ROAST TURKEY
WITH LEMON, PARSLEY AND GARLIC

SERVES 8–10

1 free-range turkey (ideally Norfolk Black or Bronze), about 5–5.5kg

sea salt and freshly ground black pepper

2 onions, peeled and halved

1 lemon, halved

1 head of garlic, halved horizontally

6 bay leaves

olive oil, to drizzle

8 rashers of smoked streaky bacon

Lemon, parsley and garlic butter:

375g butter, at room temperature

1 tbsp olive oil

finely grated zest and juice of 2 small lemons

3 garlic cloves, peeled and crushed

small bunch of flat leaf parsley, leaves only, chopped

1 Preheat the oven to 220°C/Gas 7. Meanwhile, prepare the herb butter. Put the butter into a large bowl and season with salt and pepper. Add the olive oil and mix well. Add the lemon zest and juice, crushed garlic and chopped parsley. Mix well to combine.

2 Remove the giblets from the turkey cavity. Season the cavity well with salt and pepper, then stuff with the onions, lemon, garlic halves and 2 bay leaves.

3 With your hands, loosen the skin on the breast from both ends of the bird so that you will be able to stuff the flavoured butter underneath it, making sure you keep the skin intact. Repeat with the skin on the legs – from the lower side of the breast feel your way under the skin and out towards the leg, loosening the gap.

4 Stuff half the butter mix into the opened spaces under the skin. From the outside of the skin, gently massage the butter around the breasts so that the meat is evenly covered. Finally, insert the rest of the bay leaves under the skin of the breasts.

5 Place the bird in a large roasting tray, breast side up. Spread the rest of the butter all over the skin. Season well with salt and pepper, then drizzle with a little olive oil. (If preparing a day ahead, cover the turkey with foil and refrigerate at this stage.)

6 Roast the turkey in the hot oven for 10–15 minutes. Take the tray out of the oven, baste the bird with the pan juices and lay the bacon rashers over the breast to keep it moist. Baste again. Lower the setting to 180°C/Gas 4 and cook for about 2½ hours (calculating at 30 minutes per kg), basting occasionally.

7 To test whether your turkey is cooked, insert a skewer into the thickest part of the leg and check that the juices are running clear, rather than pink. As oven temperatures and turkey shapes and sizes vary, it is crucial to check your turkey about 30 minutes before the calculated roasting time. If the juices are pink, roast for another 15 minutes and check again. Repeat as necessary until the turkey is cooked.

8 Transfer the turkey to a warmed platter and remove the parson's nose, wings and tips of the drumsticks; reserve these for the gravy. Leave the turkey to rest in a warm place for at least 45 minutes; make the gravy in the meantime. Remove the bay leaves from under the skin before carving. Serve the turkey with the piping hot gravy, stuffing and accompaniments.

This is my favourite way to roast turkey – with a savoury butter under the skin to keep the breast meat moist and flavourful. And to ensure both the turkey and pork stuffing are cooked properly, I bake the stuffing separately. Another of my secrets is to rest the turkey for a couple of hours or more. As it relaxes, the juices are re-absorbed, making the meat succulent, tender and easier to carve. It may seem like a long time, but the texture will be improved the longer you leave the turkey to rest. Piping hot gravy will restore the heat.

TURKEY GRAVY WITH CIDER AND WALNUTS

SERVES 8–10

bacon, onions, lemon and trimmings from the roast turkey
  (see left)
3 rosemary sprigs
3 tomatoes, chopped
1 litre good-quality dry cider
600ml good-quality chicken stock
2 tbsp walnut pieces, toasted
sea salt and freshly ground black pepper

1 Once you've transferred the cooked turkey to a platter to rest, drain off most of the fat from the roasting tray and place on the hob.
2 Roughly chop the bacon, add to the tray and fry for a few minutes. Chop the onions and lemon and add to the tray with 2 rosemary sprigs and the tomatoes. Cook for 1–2 minutes, then add the turkey wings, parson's nose and drumstick tips and fry for a few more minutes.
3 Pour in the cider and boil for a few minutes. Add the juices from the resting turkey and simmer to reduce the liquid by half. Pour in the stock, return to the boil, then reduce the heat slightly. Using a potato masher, crush the vegetables in the tray. Simmer for 15–20 minutes, stirring occasionally, until reduced again by a third. Take off the heat.
4 Strain the gravy through a sieve into a saucepan, pressing down on the solids in the sieve with a ladle to extract as much of the flavourful juice as possible. Add a fresh sprig of rosemary to the pan, then turn off the heat and leave to infuse for a few minutes.
5 Before serving, remove the rosemary and reheat the gravy. Coarsely crush the walnut pieces using a pestle and mortar and then tip into a warmed gravy jug. Pour the piping hot gravy on top and serve at once.

PORK, APRICOT AND PISTACHIO STUFFING

SERVES 6–8

500g pork mince
sea salt and freshly ground black pepper
1 large Braeburn apple
6 dried apricots, about 50g, chopped
30g pistachio nuts, roughly chopped
finely grated zest of 1 lemon
small bunch flat leaf parsley, leaves only, chopped
olive oil, to drizzle
large bunch of large sage leaves
2 fresh merguez or chorizo sausages

1 Preheat the oven to 200°C/Gas 6. Put the pork mince into a large bowl and season. Grate the apple into the bowl, avoiding the core. Add the apricots, pistachios, lemon zest and chopped parsley, and mix well.
2 Lay a large sheet of foil on a surface, oil with a drizzle of olive oil. Arrange the sage leaves on the foil, overlapping them in two rows to form a large rectangle, the length of the two sausages placed end to end. Sprinkle with a little seasoning.
3 Spread half of the pork stuffing mixture in the middle, along the length of the sage leaves, then run your finger down the centre of the stuffing to create a hollow for the sausages. Lay the sausages in the hollow and cover with the remaining stuffing mixture.
4 Bring up the foil and envelop the stuffing, twisting the ends to seal. Holding both ends, roll the stuffing in the foil to get a tight and even log. (Refrigerate at this stage if making a day ahead.)
5 Put the stuffing parcel into a baking dish and cook for about 40 minutes. To check if it is cooked, insert a skewer into the middle for 10 seconds – it should feel piping hot against your wrist. The log should also feel firm. Leave to rest for about 15 minutes before slicing to serve.

CARAMELISED CRANBERRY AND APPLE SAUCE

SERVES 10–12

150g caster sugar
2 star anise
4 green cardamom pods, lightly crushed
250g fresh cranberries
2 Braeburn apples, peeled, cored and chopped
sea salt and freshly ground black pepper
60ml ruby port
finely grated zest and juice of 1 orange

1 Put the sugar into a heavy-based pan with the star anise and cardamom pods and melt over a medium heat. Allow the melted sugar to turn a rich caramel colour, then add the cranberries and a touch of seasoning.
2 Cook briefly until the cranberries begin to soften, then add the apples and cook for 3–4 minutes, tossing frequently to coat the fruit in the caramel.
3 Pour in the port, then reduce the heat slightly and stir in the orange zest and juice. Simmer for about 10 minutes, allowing some of the cranberries to break down and thicken the sauce. Remove from the heat and discard the star anise and cardamom. Serve warm. (This can be made 3–4 days in advance and kept in the fridge.)

ROAST POTATOES WITH CHILLI AND TURMERIC

SERVES 8–10

2.5kg potatoes, such as Maris Piper
sea salt and freshly ground black pepper
1½ tsp ground turmeric
pinch of chilli flakes, to taste
4–5 tbsp olive oil (or goose or duck fat)

1 Preheat the oven to 200°C/Gas 6. Peel the potatoes, quarter lengthways and place in a large saucepan of salted cold water. Bring to the boil, then lower the heat and simmer for about 8 minutes.
2 Drain the potatoes in a colander and sprinkle with the turmeric, chilli flakes and some salt and pepper. Toss in the colander to coat evenly, then drizzle with a little of the olive oil and toss again. Leave to steam for 5 minutes.
3 Put the rest of the olive oil in a roasting tray and place in the oven for a few minutes to heat up. Carefully add the potatoes and toss to coat in the oil. Roast for 40–45 minutes, turning a few times, until crisp and golden. Drain on kitchen paper and transfer to a warmed dish to serve.

BRUSSELS SPROUTS WITH PANCETTA AND CHESTNUTS

SERVES 8–10

1kg Brussels sprouts, outer leaves removed
sea salt and freshly ground black pepper
1–2 tsp olive oil
200g pancetta, cut into lardons
200g vacuum-packed chestnuts
2 lemons

1 Trim the base of the Brussels sprouts and cut them in half lengthways. Bring a pan of salted water to the boil. Add the sprouts and blanch for 2–3 minutes, then drain well.
2 Heat the olive oil in a wide frying pan and fry the pancetta for a few minutes until golden and crisp. Toss in the sprouts and cook for 2–3 minutes, tossing occasionally.
3 Roughly chop the chestnuts and add them to the pan. Grate the lemon zest over the sprouts and chestnuts and squeeze over a little juice. Check the seasoning and adjust if necessary. Transfer to a warmed serving dish.

LIGHT STEAMED PUDDING
WITH WHISKEY CREAM

SERVES 6

210g butter, softened, plus extra to grease

finely grated zest of 1 orange

3 tbsp maple syrup, plus optional extra
   to drizzle

3 bay leaves

210g light brown soft sugar

4 large eggs, lightly beaten

100g self-raising flour

1½ tsp baking powder

1 tsp ground cloves

pinch of fine sea salt

Whiskey cream:

150ml double cream

dash of whiskey, to taste, plus extra
   to flambé

dash of Irish cream liqueur, to taste

1 Grease a 1.2 litre pudding basin with butter, scatter the orange zest in the bottom and pour the maple syrup on top. Put the bay leaves in the middle and press down.

2 Using an electric mixer, cream the butter and sugar together until pale and light. With the motor running on low speed, slowly add the beaten eggs, making sure each addition is incorporated before the next is added. Sift in the flour, baking powder, ground cloves and salt and fold through with a large metal spoon.

3 Spoon the mixture into the pudding basin. Lay a buttered and pleated sheet of greaseproof paper on top of the bowl, buttered side down, and cover with a sheet of pleated foil of the same size. Secure tightly with string under the rim of the bowl.

4 Stand the basin on a trivet or an upturned ramekin in a large saucepan. Pour in enough boiling water to come halfway up the side of the basin and bring to a simmer. Cover with a tight-fitting lid and simmer over a low heat for 1½ hours, checking the water level every 30 minutes or so and topping up with boiling water as needed.

5 Meanwhile, for the whiskey cream, whisk the cream with a dash each of whiskey and cream liqueur in a large bowl to soft peaks. Transfer to a serving bowl.

6 To check that the pudding is ready, unwrap and insert a skewer into the middle; it should come out clean. To unmould, loosen the sides of the sponge, then invert a warmed serving plate over the hot pudding and turn both over to unmould the pudding onto the plate. Glaze with some more maple syrup, if you wish.

7 To flambé the pudding, warm a little whiskey in a small pan and ignite it at the table with a match, then pour on top of the pudding. Serve with the whiskey cream.

After the turkey with all its trimmings and accompaniments, I find this is much more popular than the traditional heavily fruited Christmas pudding – and the whiskey cream is irresistible. You can still impress everyone with a flaming pudding, too.

BEEF WELLINGTON MENU

Pan-fried scallops with caper, raisin and olive vinaigrette

Christmas beef Wellington
Watercress purée
Truffle mashed potatoes

Pannacotta with pomegranate glaze

PLANNING YOUR TIME

WELL IN ADVANCE ...
• Order the scallops and beef fillet.

THE DAY BEFORE ...
• Prepare the beef Wellington. Sear the beef and brush with mustard. While it cools, make the mushroom duxelles. Leave to cool.
• Envelop the beef in the duxelles and Parma ham slices. Wrap in the cling film and chill to set the shape for 15–20 minutes.
• Make the watercress purée. Cool, cover and refrigerate overnight.
• Roll out the pastry and envelop the beef. Wrap in cling film and refrigerate overnight.
• Boil the potatoes for the truffle mash; drain, mash and beat in the infused creamy milk and cream. Cool, cover and refrigerate overnight.
• Make the pannacotta and chill to set.

1½ HOURS AHEAD ...
• Make the pomegranate glaze, pour into a jug and leave to cool.
• Boil the potatoes for the starter, then peel and cut into slices.
• Make the caper, raisin and olive vinaigrette.
• Preheat the oven for the beef Wellington. Brush with egg wash, score and bake for 35 minutes.

ABOUT 15 MINUTES AHEAD ...
• Put the chocolate bar for the pannacotta in the freezer.
• For the starter, fry the sliced potatoes and keep warm. Sauté the scallops and dress the salad leaves. Plate the starter.

JUST BEFORE SERVING ...
• Rest the beef Wellington while you eat the starter.
• Reheat the watercress purée.
• Reheat the mashed potatoes, adding an extra splash of milk or cream if needed. Add the butter and truffle shavings or infused oil.
• Cut the beef Wellington into thick slices and serve with the watercress purée and truffle mash.
• Pour the pomegranate glaze over each pannacotta and top with the chocolate shavings to serve.

PAN-FRIED SCALLOPS
WITH CAPER, RAISIN
AND OLIVE VINAIGRETTE

SERVES 4

250g medium new potatoes, scrubbed

sea salt and freshly ground black pepper

2–3 tbsp olive oil, plus extra to drizzle

12 large king scallops, shelled and cleaned

70g mixed baby salad leaves

squeeze of lemon juice

Caper, raisin and olive vinaigrette:

25g capers, rinsed and drained

25g raisins

25g green olives, pitted

100ml water

1 tbsp white balsamic vinegar or white
   wine vinegar

3 tbsp extra virgin olive oil

1 Cook the potatoes in a pan of salted water for 12–15 minutes until just tender. Drain and leave until cool enough to handle, then peel away the skins and slice into 5mm thick rounds. Set aside.

2 For the vinaigrette, put the capers, raisins, olives and water into a small pan and bring to a simmer. Immediately tip into a food processor and add the vinegar, olive oil and some seasoning. Whiz until smooth.

3 When ready to serve, heat a little olive oil in a large frying pan and sauté the sliced potatoes with some salt and pepper for 2 minutes on each side, or until golden and crisp. Remove and keep warm.

4 Wipe the pan clean with kitchen paper, then heat a little more oil in it until very hot. Lightly season the scallops on both sides then sauté in the oil for about a minute on each side, until golden brown and slightly springy when pressed. Remove from the pan to a warm plate and rest for a minute.

5 Meanwhile, toss the salad leaves with a little drizzle of olive oil, a squeeze of lemon juice and a pinch each of salt and pepper. Pile a little mound in the centre of each serving plate. Surround with the pan-fried scallops and arrange the potato slices around them. Spoon over a little vinaigrette and serve immediately.

This is a slightly different version of one of my signature restaurant dishes. The vinaigrette – with green olives and a little balsamic vinegar added – is more of a thick and creamy dressing. If you have any leftover, save it to serve with steamed or roast fish. Needless to say, the scallops must be very fresh.

CHRISTMAS BEEF WELLINGTON

SERVES 4–6

900g piece beef fillet of even thickness
(from the centre cut)

sea salt and freshly ground black pepper

2 tbsp olive oil

English mustard, to brush meat

Mushroom duxelles:

700g chestnut mushrooms, cleaned
and stalks removed

handful of cooked chestnuts

1 garlic clove, peeled and chopped

2 thyme sprigs, leaves only

To assemble:

8 slices of Parma ham

500g ready-made all-butter puff pastry

plain flour, to dust

2 egg yolks, lightly beaten with 1 tbsp
water (eggwash)

1 Trim the beef of any sinew and season well with salt and pepper. Heat the olive oil in a large frying pan over a high heat, add the fillet and quickly sear the outside all over for about 5 minutes until evenly browned, turning as necessary. Transfer to a plate and while still hot, brush all over with mustard. Set aside to rest.

2 For the duxelles, put the mushrooms, chestnuts and garlic in a food processor with a little salt and pepper and blend to a fine paste, stopping to scrape down the sides a few times. Heat a dry large frying pan. Scrape the mushroom paste into the pan and add the thyme leaves. Cook over a high heat, stirring occasionally, to drive off the moisture and intensify the flavour. The duxelles must be sufficiently dry otherwise it will make the pastry soggy; the mixture should adhere easily. Spread out on a tray to cool.

3 Place a large piece of cling film on a clean surface. Lay the Parma ham slices on top, overlapping them slightly, to form a rough rectangle large enough to envelop the beef fillet, making sure there are no gaps. Season the ham with a few twists of pepper then, with a palette knife, spread the duxelles on top, leaving a 2.5cm margin along the edges.

4 Lay the beef fillet along the middle of the mushroom layer. Keeping a tight hold of the cling film from the outside edges, neatly roll the Parma ham and duxelles over the beef into a tight barrel shape. Twist the ends of the cling film to secure. Refrigerate for 15 minutes to firm up.

5 Roll out the pastry on a lightly floured surface to a large rectangle, the thickness of a £1 coin and brush with some of the eggwash. Unwrap the beef from the cling film and place it in the middle. Leaving a large enough rectangle to wrap around the beef, trim off the excess pastry. Roll the pastry around the beef to envelop it and then press the edges to seal. Pinch the pastry at the ends to seal and trim off the excess. Wrap the log tightly in cling film and chill for 10 minutes, or overnight if you are preparing ahead.

6 Preheat the oven to 190°C/Gas 5. Remove the cling film and brush the parcel all over with egg wash. Lightly score the pastry at 1cm intervals with the back of a small knife for a decorative effect, if you wish. Place on a baking tray, sprinkle with salt and bake for about 35 minutes; if the pastry appears to be browning too quickly, lower the setting slightly. Leave to rest in a warm place for about 15 minutes before cutting into thick slices to serve, with the accompaniments.

Beef Wellington is always impressive, but my updated version is a real special occasion treat. I've retained the luxurious character of the dish and, for a festive touch, added cooked chestnuts to the mushroom duxelles – for a delicious twist on an old classic. This has to be one of my all-time favourite main courses.

WATERCRESS PURÉE

SERVES 6–8
300g watercress, trimmed
150ml water
100g spinach leaves
2–3 tbsp double cream
sea salt and freshly ground black pepper

1 Wash the watercress well, then put into a large saucepan with the water and bring to the boil. Cover and cook over a medium heat for 4–5 minutes.
2 Rinse the spinach leaves, then add them to the watercress and stir well. Cook for a further minute, or just until the spinach leaves have wilted. Drain in a colander, pressing with the back of a ladle to extract as much moisture as possible.
3 Tip the watercress and spinach into a blender or food processor, add 2 tbsp cream and blend for 5–10 minutes to a very smooth purée, scraping down the sides a few times. Taste for seasoning. If you prefer the purée thinner, add another 1 tbsp cream or a tiny splash of hot water and gently reheat before serving.

TRUFFLE MASHED POTATOES

SERVES 4
1kg potatoes, such as Desirée, peeled and quartered
sea salt and freshly ground black pepper
200ml double cream
100ml whole milk
2 thyme sprigs
1 bay leaf
25g butter, in pieces, or a drizzle of truffle-infused olive oil
1 white Alba truffle (optional)

1 Add the potatoes to a pan of salted cold water, bring to the boil and cook for 15–20 minutes, until tender.
2 Meanwhile, heat the cream and milk in a small pan with the thyme sprigs, bay leaf and some seasoning. Bring to a simmer, reduce the heat and simmer gently for a few minutes. Take the pan off the heat and allow the flavours to infuse for a few minutes.
3 Once the potatoes are cooked, drain and return them to the pan. Place over a low heat for 1–2 minutes to dry them out a little. Mash the potatoes smoothly, using a potato ricer or masher into a clean pan.
4 Pour the infused cream mixture through a sieve into a jug and discard the herbs. Over a very gentle heat, gradually add the cream mixture to the mashed potatoes and beat until smooth and creamy. Once it is all added, the mash should be soft enough to just drop from the spoon.
5 Transfer the mash to a warmed serving dish and top with slithers of butter or a drizzle of truffle-infused oil (if you are not using fresh truffle). Finally, shave the white truffle on top, if using, and sprinkle with a pinch each of salt and pepper. Serve piping hot.

PANNACOTTA
WITH POMEGRANATE GLAZE

SERVES 4

2 medium sheets leaf gelatine
(11 x 7.5cm)

250ml double cream

50g caster sugar

50ml milk

15ml dark rum, or to taste

Pomegranate glaze:

20g caster sugar

275ml pomegranate juice

Chocolate shavings:

block of good-quality dark chocolate,
for grating

1 Soak the gelatine in a shallow dish of cold water for a few minutes. Meanwhile, put the cream, sugar, milk and rum into a saucepan and slowly bring to a simmer. Heat gently for 30 seconds, then remove the pan from the heat. Taste for flavour, adding a little more rum if you wish.

2 Squeeze the gelatine leaves to remove excess water, then add them to the cream mixture and stir until fully dissolved. Tip the mixture into a jug.

3 Now pour into 4 individual glass dishes, leaving enough room for the glaze. Leave to cool, then place the glasses in the fridge to set for at least 2 hours, or overnight if preparing ahead.

4 To make the pomegranate glaze, heat a dry frying pan. Tip the sugar into the hot pan followed by the pomegranate juice. Bring to the boil and allow to bubble for 10–15 minutes, until thickened to a sticky, syrupy glaze. Pour into a small jug and leave to cool completely.

5 Pop the chocolate in the freezer for 10–15 minutes before serving. Pour the cooled pomegranate glaze on top of the chilled pannacottas. Take the chocolate from the freezer and draw a small straight-edged knife along the flat side of the bar to make curled shavings. Top each pannacotta with chocolate shavings to serve.

Over Christmas, it makes sense to prepare desserts that require minimal effort yet still deliver that 'wow' factor. Pannacotta certainly ticks all the right boxes – it's easy to make, cheap and delectable, with a silky smooth texture that makes it one of the world's sexiest desserts.

GLAZED HAM MENU

Cream of cauliflower soup with truffle oil and croûtons

Honey glazed ham
Pear and saffron chutney
Parsnip purée
Creamed cabbage with thyme

Ricotta cake with caramelised clementines and star anise

PLANNING YOUR TIME

WELL IN ADVANCE . . .
• Order your gammon.
• Make the pear and saffron chutney and seal in sterilised jars.

THE DAY BEFORE . . .
• Make the cauliflower soup. Cool, cover and refrigerate.
• Fry the croûtons. Cool and store in an airtight container.
• Make the parsnip purée. Cool, cover and refrigerate.

4 HOURS AHEAD . . .
• Simmer the gammon with the vegetables and aromatics for 3 hours. (Or this can be done the day before, leaving the ham in the poaching liquid overnight.)
• Bake the ricotta cake and top with the caramelised clementines. Keep in a cool spot.

AN HOUR AHEAD . . .
• Make the honey glaze for the ham.
• Score the ham, stud with the cloves and pour over half of the glaze. Roast in the oven for 15 minutes.
• Pour on the rest of the glaze and continue to roast, basting frequently.

ABOUT 15 MINUTES AHEAD . . .
• Rest the ham.
• Prepare the creamed Savoy cabbage with thyme.
• Put the pear and saffron chutney into a serving bowl.

JUST BEFORE SERVING . . .
• Reheat the cauliflower soup. Serve topped with the truffle oil and croûtons.
• Reheat the parsnip purée and creamed cabbage.
• Carve the ham and serve with the accompaniments.
• Whip some cream to accompany the ricotta cake if required and serve.

CREAM OF CAULIFLOWER SOUP
WITH TRUFFLE OIL AND CROÛTONS

SERVES 8

1 large or 2 medium cauliflower(s), about 1.2kg

25g butter

1 tbsp olive oil

1 large potato, about 250g, peeled and roughly chopped

1 onion, peeled and chopped

1.2 litres chicken or vegetable stock

400ml whole milk

sea salt and freshly ground black pepper

100ml double cream

Croûtons:

2 tbsp olive oil or goose fat

2 slices day-old country-style bread, about 50g, cut into cubes

To finish:

truffle-infused oil, to drizzle

1 Remove the stalk from the cauliflower and then cut into florets. Heat the butter and olive oil in a large saucepan, then tip in the cauliflower florets, potato and onion. Cover and sweat for about 10 minutes over a low heat, stirring occasionally, until the vegetables are softened but not coloured.

2 Pour in the stock and bring to the boil. Add the milk with some seasoning and return to a simmer. Now simmer, uncovered, for 10–15 minutes until all of the vegetables are soft. Add the cream and remove from the heat. Purée the soup using a freestanding or hand-held stick blender until smooth.

3 For the croûtons, heat the olive oil or goose fat in a frying pan over a medium heat. Add the bread cubes and fry until golden and crisp, turning frequently. Drain on kitchen paper and sprinkle with a little sea salt.

4 Return the soup to a clean pan, check the seasoning and reheat gently. Ladle into warmed bowls, drizzle over a little truffle oil and scatter a few croûtons on top. Serve immediately.

A comforting, creamy soup – perfect for this time of the year. As a starter to a three-course Christmas menu, you will only need to serve a small portion, but this is also a great warming soup to have for lunch with some good bread after a walk on a wintry day.

HONEY GLAZED HAM

SERVES 8–10

3kg unsmoked boneless gammon joint

4 medium carrots, peeled and roughly chopped

1 leek, cleaned and roughly chopped

1 onion, peeled and roughly chopped

1 tsp black peppercorns, lightly crushed

1 tsp coriander seeds, lightly crushed

1 cinnamon stick, broken in half

3 bay leaves

handful of cloves

Honey glaze:

100g demerara sugar

50ml Madeira

25ml sherry vinegar

125g honey

1 Put the gammon into a large saucepan and pour on enough cold water to cover. Add the carrots, leek, onion, peppercorns, coriander seeds, cinnamon stick and bay leaves. Bring to the boil, turn down to a simmer and cook for 3 hours, topping up with more boiling water if necessary. Skim off the froth and any impurities that rise to the surface from time to time. If cooking in advance, leave the ham to cool in the stock overnight. Otherwise, allow it to cool a little, then remove from the pan. Strain the stock (and save for soups, sauces, etc.).

2 To make the glaze, put the sugar, Madeira, sherry vinegar and honey into a pan and stir over a low heat. Bring to the boil, lower the heat and simmer for 3–4 minutes, until you have a glossy dark syrup. Do not leave unattended, as it can easily boil over.

3 Preheat the oven to 190°C/Gas 5. Lift the ham onto a board. Snip and remove the string and then cut away the skin from the ham, leaving behind an even layer of fat. Lightly score the fat all over in a criss-cross, diamond pattern, taking care not to cut into the meat. Stud the centre of each diamond with a clove.

4 Put the ham into a roasting tin and pour half of the glaze over the surface. Roast for 15 minutes.

5 Pour on the rest of the glaze and return to the oven for another 25–35 minutes until the ham is golden brown, basting with the pan juices frequently. It also helps to turn the pan as you baste to ensure that the joint colours evenly.

6 Remove from the oven and leave to rest for 15 minutes before carving and serving with the accompaniments.

A lovely glazed ham is a great staple over Christmas, not least because it's also delicious cold with my pear and saffron chutney. Roast on the day if serving hot, or up to 2 days ahead if serving cold. Any leftover ham can be used in a variety of dishes (see my suggestions on pages 114–15) and please don't throw away the ham stock – it is great for soups, stews, risottos and sauces, so freeze it in convenient batches.

PEAR AND SAFFRON CHUTNEY

MAKES 2–3 MEDIUM JARS

1 tbsp olive oil

1 small onion, peeled and chopped

sea salt and freshly ground black pepper

50g knob of fresh root ginger, peeled and finely grated

pinch of freshly grated nutmeg

1 tsp ground cinnamon

½ –1 tsp cayenne pepper, to taste

250g light unrefined soft brown sugar

250ml white wine vinegar

4 firm pears (such as Williams), about 650g

1 small cooking apple, about 350g, peeled, cored and chopped

125g sultanas

2 pinches of saffron strands

finely grated zest and juice of 2 small oranges

2 tomatoes, diced

1 Heat the olive oil in a large pan, add the onion and sweat for a few minutes with a touch of seasoning, to soften but not colour. Add the grated ginger, nutmeg, cinnamon and cayenne pepper. Sauté for another 1–2 minutes. Add the sugar and stir over a medium heat until it has dissolved, then add the wine vinegar.

2 Peel, core and chop the pears and apple. Add to the pan with the sultanas, saffron and orange zest and juice. Bring to the boil and boil steadily for about 15 minutes, until the liquid has reduced down to a syrupy consistency.

3 Add the diced tomatoes and cook for a few minutes, by which time the chutney should be well reduced and thickened. Taste and adjust the seasoning with a little salt and pepper.

4 While still hot, spoon the chutney into clean, sterilised jars and seal. Store in a cool, dark cupboard or the fridge and use within 6 months – the flavour will improve with time.

This is an amazing, piquant relish that works wonderfully with the aromatic glazed ham. It has layers of flavours and textures, plus a little saffron to give it a luxurious colour and taste.

PARSNIP PURÉE

SERVES 8

1kg parsnips, about 8–10 large ones
75g butter
sea salt and freshly ground black pepper
200ml double cream

1 Peel and cut the parsnips into roughly even dice. Melt the butter in a saucepan over a low heat and add the parsnips with some salt and pepper. Give them a stir, then cover and sweat gently for about 20 minutes, stirring occasionally, until they are very soft and you can squash them with a wooden spoon. Pour in the cream and bring to the boil.
2 Immediately tip the contents of the pan into a blender or food processor and whiz to a smooth purée. Check the seasoning. Return to the pan, ready to reheat to serve.

CREAMED CABBAGE WITH THYME

SERVES 8

50g butter
1 large garlic clove, peeled and crushed
few thyme sprigs, leaves only
1 large or 2 small Savoy cabbage(s), finely shredded
200ml vegetable stock or water
90 ml double cream

1 Melt the butter in a large pan and add the garlic and thyme leaves. Fry for 30 seconds, then stir in the shredded cabbage. Sauté for about 5 minutes until the cabbage starts to wilt.
2 Pour in the stock or water and simmer for about 5 minutes, until the liquid has evaporated and the cabbage is tender. Stir in the cream. Transfer to a warmed bowl to serve.

RICOTTA CAKE
WITH CARAMELISED CLEMENTINES
AND STAR ANISE

SERVES 8

140g unsalted butter, at room
    temperature, plus extra to grease

plain flour, to dust

140g caster sugar

375g ricotta

3 medium eggs, separated,
    plus 2 extra egg yolks

finely grated zest of 3 clementines,
    plus 3 tbsp juice

175g self-raising flour, sifted

1 tsp baking powder

pinch of fine sea salt

Caramelised clementines:

4–5 seedless clementines

100g caster sugar

4 star anise

75ml clementine juice
    or orange liqueur, such as
    Grand Marnier or Cointreau

To serve (optional):

whipped cream

1 Preheat the oven to 160°C/Gas 2½. Lightly butter a 23–24cm springform cake tin and dust with flour.

2 Cream the butter and sugar together using an electric whisk until pale and fluffy. Whisk in the ricotta, the 5 egg yolks and the clementine zest and juice until evenly combined. Sift the flour, baking powder and salt together into another bowl.

3 In a clean bowl (with clean beaters), whisk the egg whites to stiff peaks. In alternate batches, fold the egg whites and sifted flour mix into the ricotta mixture until evenly combined. Transfer the mixture to the prepared cake tin and bake for 50–60 minutes, until risen and a skewer inserted into the middle comes out clean.

4 Ten minutes before the cake will be cooked, make the topping. Peel the clementines, removing all pith, then slice crosswise into 1cm rounds and remove the pips.

5 Put the sugar and star anise into a dry heavy-based pan over a high heat. When the sugar begins to melt and caramelise, tilt the pan to swirl the syrup so that it colours evenly. As soon as it reaches a terracotta brown colour, add the clementine juice or liqueur, standing well back as the hot caramel will splutter. Some of it will harden on contact with the juice, so stir over a medium heat until it melts to a thick, glossy caramel. Remove from the heat, add the clementines and toss to coat in the caramel.

6 Once the cake is ready, remove from the oven and leave to cool for about 15 minutes (it will sink slightly on cooling). Carefully unmould and transfer it to a serving plate or cake stand. While the cake is still warm, lightly prick the surface all over with a skewer then drizzle over some of the caramel. Arrange the clementine slices on top and drizzle over the rest of the caramel. Leave to cool completely.

7 Slice the cake to serve and accompany with whipped cream if you like.

Brimming with Christmassy clementines, this is a moist, dense cake, with a subtle hint of star anise. The cake itself freezes well in a sealed container. Once topped with the barely cooked clementines and syrup, it is best eaten within a day, or over a couple of days at most.

SEA BASS MENU

Smoked duck breast salad with pomegranate vinaigrette

Pan-fried sea bass with lemongrass velouté
Potato and celeriac dauphinoise
Broccoli or sugar snap peas

Sherry-glazed figs with pine nut brittle

PLANNING YOUR TIME

WELL IN ADVANCE ...
- Order the smoked duck breast from your butcher or delicatessen.
- Order the sea bass fillets from your fishmonger.

THE DAY BEFORE ...
- Make the pine nut brittle. Store in an airtight container.
- Prepare the lemongrass velouté, cool and refrigerate.

1½ HOURS AHEAD ...
- Assemble and bake the potato and celeriac dauphinoise.
- Make the pomegranate vinaigrette.

ABOUT 15 MINUTES AHEAD ...
- Thinly slice the duck breasts and combine the salad leaves in a bowl.

JUST BEFORE SERVING ...
- Toss the salad leaves in the vinaigrette, plate the salad and serve the starter.
- Blanch the broccoli or sugar snap peas.
- Reheat the lemongrass velouté. Score and fry the sea bass fillets. Serve with the dauphinoise and green vegetable.
- Cook and glaze the figs, then serve with the pine nut brittle.

SMOKED DUCK BREAST SALAD
WITH POMEGRANATE VINAIGRETTE

SERVES 4

1 large smoked duck breast, about 330g

1 large head of chicory

100g rocket leaves

handful of small basil leaves, shredded
   (optional)

seeds from ½ pomegranate

2–3 tbsp flaked almonds, toasted

Pomegranate vinaigrette:

2 tbsp pomegranate molasses

1 tbsp hot water

1 tsp Dijon mustard

3 tbsp extra virgin olive oil

3 tbsp groundnut oil

sea salt and freshly ground black pepper

1 First, make the pomegranate vinaigrette. Whisk together the pomegranate molasses, water and mustard, then add the oils and whisk thoroughly to combine. Season with salt and pepper to taste.

2 Thinly slice the duck breast and set aside. Trim the base from the chicory and separate into leaves. Cut the large outer leaves into quarters and the smaller ones in half. Place in a large bowl. Add the rocket and basil, if using, and toss with a few tablespoonfuls of the vinaigrette.

3 Arrange the salad and duck breast slices attractively on individual serving plates, then scatter the pomegranate seeds and toasted almonds over each salad. Drizzle with more pomegranate vinaigrette to serve.

This is one of the easiest dishes in the book, as it doesn't require any cooking – merely a few minutes to assemble. Pomegranate molasses, available in Middle Eastern grocers and some larger supermarkets, has a slightly sweet tang and is lovely in the vinaigrette.

PAN-FRIED SEA BASS
WITH LEMONGRASS VELOUTÉ

SERVES 4

4 sea bass fillets, skin on, about 175g each

olive oil, to cook

sea salt and freshly ground black pepper

few knobs of butter

Lemongrass velouté:

knob of unsalted butter

2 large shallots, peeled and finely
    chopped

200ml dry white wine or vermouth

500ml fish or chicken stock

1 lemongrass stalk, trimmed and
    roughly chopped

200ml double cream

1 First, make the lemongrass velouté. Heat the butter in a wide pan. Add the shallots and fry gently for 5–10 minutes, until softened but not coloured. Pour in the wine or vermouth, bring to the boil and let it bubble vigorously until reduced by two-thirds.

2 Add the stock and lemongrass to the sauce and return to the boil. Reduce by half, then pour in the cream. Bring the sauce to a simmer and let simmer until reduced and thickened to the consistency of pouring cream. Season to taste with salt and pepper, then pass the sauce through a fine sieve into a jug or bowl. (You can prepare the sauce to this stage up to 2 days ahead; cool and refrigerate until needed.)

3 Check the sea bass fillets for small pin bones, removing any you find with tweezers. Score the skin lightly at regular intervals with the tip of a sharp knife. Heat a little olive oil in a large non-stick frying pan until hot. Season the fish fillets on both sides with salt and pepper, then place in the pan, skin side down. (You may have to cook the fish in 2 batches, depending on the size of your pan.)

4 Fry the fish without moving for 2–3 minutes, adding a few knobs of butter after a minute and basting frequently with the hot oil and butter as it cooks. When the fish is cooked two-thirds of the way through and the skin is golden and crisp, flip the fillets over and cook the other side briefly, for about 30 seconds, basting with the butter.

5 Spoon the velouté onto warmed plates and lay the sea bass fillets on top, skin side up. Serve immediately with the potato and celeriac dauphinoise (see page 71) and some tender stem broccoli or sugar snap peas.

This restaurant-style dish is sure to impress your friends and family. It is ideal if you are entertaining a smaller number and do not want to have lots of leftovers, as you would with a roast turkey. Make the lemongrass velouté the day before and you'll only need 5 minutes or so on the day to fry the fish and reheat the sauce before serving.

POTATO AND CELERIAC DAUPHINOISE

SERVES 4

butter, to grease

120ml double cream

120ml whole milk

1 bay leaf

2 garlic cloves, peeled and smashed

400g celeriac

400g waxy potatoes, such as Desirée

sea salt and freshly ground black pepper

1–2 tbsp hazelnut oil

75g medium Cheddar, grated

1 Preheat the oven to 180°C/Gas 4. Lightly butter a deep 1-litre gratin dish. Put the cream, milk, bay leaf and garlic in a pan and heat until simmering. When the liquid begins to bubble up the sides of the pan, turn off the heat and leave to cool slightly.
2 Peel and quarter the celeriac, then slice as thinly as you can, preferably using a mandolin. Peel and thinly slice the potatoes. Put the celeriac and potato slices in a large bowl, season generously with salt and pepper and then toss with the hazelnut oil.
3 Layer the celeriac and potato slices in the gratin dish, overlapping them slightly. Strain the creamy milk, discarding the bay and garlic, then pour over the celeriac and potato until it reaches just below the top layer; gently press down on the slices. Bake for 45–50 minutes, until the potatoes and celeriac are tender when pierced with a knife.
4 Take the dish out the oven and scatter the cheese over the surface. Bake for a further 10–15 minutes until golden and crisp. Leave the dauphinoise to stand for a few minutes before serving.

The addition of celeriac to this dauphinoise makes it a slightly lighter version of the classic potato dish. Apart from the sea bass, it also makes a delicious accompaniment to roast poultry, lamb or beef, or you could serve it for lunch with a side salad and cold meats.

SHERRY GLAZED FIGS
WITH PINE NUT BRITTLE

SERVES 4

8 large figs

1–2 tbsp caster sugar

25g unsalted butter

125ml Pedro Ximénez sherry

Pine nut brittle:

100g caster sugar

100g pine nuts

To serve:

crème fraîche

1 First, make the pine nut brittle. Have ready a baking sheet lined with a non-stick silicone mat. Put the sugar into a dry frying pan and place over a medium-high heat. Without stirring, let the sugar dissolve and begin to caramelise. Swirl the pan to ensure that the caramel colours evenly. When it turns a terracotta brown colour, add the pine nuts and swirl to coat. Pour onto the silicone mat and tilt the baking sheet to spread the mixture thinly (or use a heatproof spatula). Leave to cool completely and harden.

2 Once cooled, break the pine nut brittle up into small pieces. (It can be made several days in advance and stored in an airtight container.)

3 Ten minutes before serving, prepare the figs. Trim the tops, halve vertically, then sprinkle the cut surfaces with a little sugar. Melt the butter in a wide frying pan over a high heat. As it begins to foam, add the figs, cut side down, and cook for 2–3 minutes until the sugar dissolves and caramelises.

4 Pour in the sherry and simmer for about 30 seconds. Carefully transfer the figs to a warmed plate, leaving the sherry in the pan. Boil the sherry until reduced by half to a light syrupy glaze.

5 Divide the glazed figs among individual plates and drizzle over the sherry glaze. Add some pine nut brittle and a neat spoonful of crème fraîche. Serve immediately.

A light and original dessert, this is truly delicious. The nut brittle – which can also be made with slivered almonds or roughly broken hazelnuts – adds a lovely contrasting crunch to the figs and caramel, and it can be made in advance. The figs should be glazed just before eating, but this will only take a few minutes.

ROAST GOOSE MENU

Roast goose with five spice and honey
Redcurrant and red wine sauce
Braised red cabbage and apple
Honey glazed carrots and parsnips

Passion fruit parfait

PLANNING YOUR TIME

WELL IN ADVANCE ...
• Order your goose.
• Prepare the braised red cabbage and apple. Keep refrigerated.

THE DAY BEFORE ...
• Make the passion fruit parfait and freeze it.
• For the sauce, reduce the stock, wine, port and vinegar. Keep in the fridge.

5–6 HOURS IN ADVANCE ...
• Bring the goose to room temperature.

2½ HOURS AHEAD ...
• Prepare the goose for roasting and put in the oven.
• Peel the carrots and parsnips and keep them immersed in chilled water.

AN HOUR AHEAD ...
• Keep an eye on the goose, basting well and checking for doneness.

ABOUT 30 MINUTES AHEAD ...
• Rest the goose.

ABOUT 15 MINUTES AHEAD ...
• Reheat the braised red cabbage and apple.
• Sauté the carrots and parsnips.
• Reheat the reduced liquor for the sauce.

JUST BEFORE SERVING ...
• Finish cooking the carrots and parsnips.
• Add the redcurrant jelly and fresh redcurrants to the sauce.
• Carve the goose and serve with the accompaniments.
• Unmould the passion fruit parfait and decorate.

ROAST GOOSE
WITH FIVE SPICE AND HONEY

SERVES 6–8

5.5–6.5kg oven-ready goose

2 oranges, finely grated zest and fruit cut into wedges

2 lemons, finely grated zest and fruit cut into wedges

2 tbsp Chinese five-spice powder

1 tbsp good-quality sea salt

freshly ground black pepper

4–5 tbsp runny honey, to drizzle

1 Preheat the oven to 220°C/Gas 7 and place a deep roasting pan fitted with a rack in the oven to heat up. If the goose is ready-trussed, remove the string and gently tug and loosen the legs and wings a little – this helps the bird to cook more evenly. Remove the giblets from the body cavity and trim off any excess fat from the neck and cavity.

2 In a small bowl, mix the orange and lemon zest with the five-spice powder, salt and pepper. Lightly score the skin of the goose in a criss-cross pattern with a sharp knife, taking care not to cut into the flesh. Rub the seasoning all over the skin and inside the cavity of the goose. Put the orange and lemon wedges into the cavity. (You can prepare to this stage a day ahead and refrigerate the goose.)

3 Place the goose on the rack in the preheated roasting pan, breast side up, and roast for 15 minutes. Turn the setting down to 170°C/Gas 3 and roast for another 30 minutes.

4 Take the goose out of the oven and pour off some of the fat from the roasting tin (save for roasting potatoes). Drizzle the honey over the goose, put back in the oven and roast for another 30 minutes – 1 hour, basting once or twice. Cover loosely with foil if it is browning too much towards the end of cooking. For medium-rare meat, the flesh should feel firm with a slight spring when lightly pressed; a meat thermometer inserted into the thickest part of a thigh (but not touching a bone) should register 70°C. Also, bear in mind that the bird will continue to cook in its own heat during resting.

5 Remove the goose from the oven and cover loosely with foil. Let it rest for 30 minutes.

6 Carve the goose and serve with the sauce and accompaniments.

To me, this is the ultimate way to roast a goose and the aromatic five-spice powder really lifts the flavour of the rich, gamey meat. Unlike turkey, you want to cook goose to medium rare for the best texture. It is important to check the bird half an hour before the end of the estimated cooking time, as the size, density and fat ratio can all make a difference. Thereafter, keep checking on the goose every 15 minutes or so.

REDCURRANT AND RED WINE SAUCE

SERVES 6–8
800ml good-quality chicken stock
300ml red wine
75ml ruby port
2½ tbsp balsamic vinegar
125g redcurrants
2½ tbsp redcurrant jelly
sea salt and freshly ground black pepper

1 To make the sauce, pour the stock, wine, port and balsamic vinegar into a saucepan and boil vigorously for about 20 minutes, until reduced by two-thirds or thickened to a light syrupy consistency (this can be done up to 3 days ahead).
2 Add the redcurrants and redcurrant jelly to the pan and simmer for 2–3 minutes, until the redcurrants are just starting to burst. Season with salt and pepper to taste. Reheat before serving if necessary.

BRAISED RED CABBAGE AND APPLE

SERVES 6–8
1 small red cabbage, about 600–700g
1 large Bramley apple
50g butter
50g dark brown sugar
50ml good-quality red wine vinegar
400ml soft, fruity red wine
300ml good-quality chicken stock
3 bay leaves
3 star anise
6–8 cloves
sea salt and freshly ground black pepper

1 Preheat the oven to 180°C/Gas 4. Quarter, core and finely shred the red cabbage. Peel, core and thickly slice the apple. Put the butter, sugar, wine vinegar, wine and stock into a large ovenproof casserole dish and stir over a medium heat until the sugar has dissolved.
2 Add the bay leaves, star anise, cloves and a good pinch each of salt and pepper. Tip in the cabbage and apple and stir well. Bring to the boil, then put the lid on and place in the oven.
3 Bake for an hour, stirring halfway, then uncover and return to the oven for another 15 minutes, or until the cabbage is tender. (This dish can be prepared ahead and kept in the fridge for up to 3 days; reheat to serve.)

HONEY GLAZED CARROTS AND PARSNIPS

SERVES 6–8
500g parsnips
500g carrots
2–3 tbsp olive oil
few thyme sprigs
1 cinnamon stick, broken in two
3 star anise
sea salt and freshly ground black pepper
1–2 tbsp clear honey
splash of water
few knobs of butter

1 Peel and halve or quarter the parsnips and carrots so that the pieces are of a similar size.
2 Heat the olive oil in a large sauté pan, then add the carrots and parsnips and toss to coat in the oil. Add the thyme, cinnamon, star anise and some seasoning. Cook over a medium heat for 15–20 minutes, turning the vegetables frequently, until golden brown and almost cooked through.
3 Drizzle over the honey and cook until the vegetables start to caramelise. Deglaze the pan with the water and increase the heat. Cook for 2–3 minutes, until the liquid has evaporated and the carrots and parsnips are cooked through. Stir through a few knobs of butter to glaze.

PASSION FRUIT PARFAIT

SERVES 6

8 ripe large passion fruit

sunflower oil, to oil

6 large egg yolks

75g caster sugar

50ml water

2 tbsp vodka

300ml double cream

To finish:

long, thin mango slices

seeds from 1 passion fruit

1 Halve the passion fruit, scoop out the pulp and seeds into a sieve set over a small pan and press to extract the juice. Bring the juice to the boil and let bubble until reduced by half, to 60–70ml. Set aside to cool. Lightly oil 6 darioles or other individual moulds.

2 Beat the egg yolks in a heatproof medium bowl using a hand-held electric whisk until light and fluffy. Set the bowl over a pan of simmering water and continue to whisk until pale, stiff and at least doubled in volume. Take the bowl off the heat.

3 Put the sugar and water in a small saucepan and stir over a low heat until the sugar has dissolved, then stop stirring and boil vigorously until the temperature registers 110°C on a sugar thermometer. The syrup should be thick with large bubbles.

4 Briefly whisk the egg yolk mixture again, then still whisking, slowly trickle in the sugar syrup. Once incorporated, the mixture will be thick, glossy and mousse-like. Continue to whisk for another 5 minutes, or until the side of the bowl no longer feels hot. Fold in the passion fruit purée and vodka. Cover the bowl with cling film and place in the fridge for an hour.

5 Whip the cream until softly peaking, then carefully fold into the passion fruit mixture. Spoon into the prepared moulds and set on a tray. Freeze for 2–3 hours until firm, or overnight.

6 To turn out each parfait, wipe a hot cloth around the mould (or dip into a bowl of hot water for a second or two). Invert the mould onto a plate and give it a light shake to release the parfait. Top each parfait with a folded mango slice or two and a few passion fruit seeds to serve.

This is a fabulously refreshing dessert to end a rich meal. Topped with fine slices of mango and passion fruit seeds, these individual parfaits look particularly stunning, but you can also set the parfait in a small loaf tin lined with cling film. To serve, turn out and cut into slices using a warm knife.

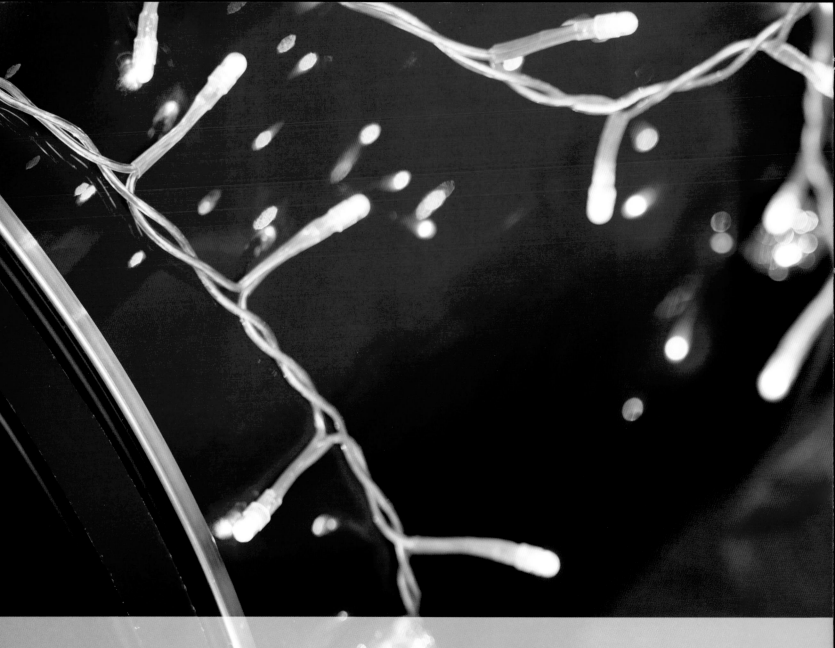

BREAKFAST & BRUNCH

CHRISTMAS MUESLI

MAKES ABOUT 1.3KG

400g porridge oats

75g unsweetened desiccated coconut

100g skinned hazelnuts

100g skinned Brazil nuts, roughly
  chopped

100g soft light brown sugar

1 tsp ground cinnamon or mixed spice

1 tsp ground ginger

180ml water

120ml groundnut oil

½ tsp vanilla extract

½ tsp fine sea salt

75g pitted dates, roughly chopped

75g dried apricots, roughly chopped

75g dried cranberries

50g crystallised ginger, finely chopped
  (optional)

1 Preheat the oven to 170°C/Gas 3. Combine the oats, coconut, hazelnuts, Brazil nuts, brown sugar and ground spices in a large bowl. Mix well.

2 Whisk together the water, oil, vanilla and salt and then stir into the dry ingredients.

3 Spread the mixture out in two large, shallow roasting trays. Roast in the oven for 20–30 minutes, stirring and swapping the trays occasionally, until the muesli is golden and crisp, checking frequently towards the end. Leave to cool.

4 Stir in the dried fruit and crystallised ginger. Store in an airtight container.

Clusters of lightly spiced porridge oats and coconut with roasted nuts and an assortment of dried fruits make a lovely Christmas breakfast. Enjoy the muesli plainly with milk, or use it to top Greek yoghurt and have with my fig and apple compote. For an original foodie gift, pack in cellophane bags and pop into a gift bag with a jar of the compote.

FIG AND APPLE COMPOTE

Dissolve 275g granulated sugar in 350ml water in a wide, medium saucepan over a low heat, then add a cinnamon stick, 5 cloves and the thinly pared zest of 1 orange. Boil rapidly for 2–3 minutes, then add 50ml brandy. Peel, core and quarter 3 dessert apples, then cut into thick wedges. Add to the pan and simmer for 8–10 minutes, covered with a crumpled piece of greaseproof paper. Trim and halve 8 figs, add to the pan and simmer for a further 3–4 minutes, until the fruit is just softened but holding its shape. While still hot, transfer to sterilised jars and seal. When cool, store in the fridge for up to 1 month. Once opened, consume within a week. Enjoy with a bowl of muesli-topped yoghurt or pancakes.
8–10 SERVINGS

CHESTNUT MUFFINS

MAKES 12

200g chestnut flour or spelt flour

75g plain flour

1⅓ tsp baking powder

3 tbsp medium oats, plus extra to
   sprinkle

125g caster sugar

250g tin sweetened chestnut purée
   (crème de marron)

3 medium eggs, lightly beaten

5 tbsp milk

100ml groundnut or vegetable oil

demerara sugar, to sprinkle (optional)

1 Preheat the oven to 170°C/Gas 3. Line a 12-hole muffin tin with paper cases. Sift the flours and baking powder into a large bowl and stir in the oats and caster sugar. Make a well in the middle.

2 Put the chestnut purée into another bowl and beat for a minute to loosen it. Mix in the eggs, milk and oil until evenly combined, then pour into the dry ingredients. Using a large metal spoon, fold together as lightly as possible. Avoid over-mixing for the best result; a few lumps of flour are preferable to over-working.

3 Spoon the mixture into the muffin cases and sprinkle with oats and demerara sugar, if using. Bake for 25–30 minutes, or until risen and golden; a skewer inserted into the middle should come out clean.

4 Transfer the muffins to a wire rack to cool.

These muffins taste best freshly baked, but you can make them a day ahead and warm them in a hot oven for 5 minutes before serving. For a teatime treat, top the cooled muffins with vanilla frosting and pieces of marron glacé.

CHRISTMAS SMOOTHIE

Peel, core and roughly chop 4 ripe pears. Put them into a blender and add 1–2 tbsp maple syrup, 5 heaped tbsp Greek or natural yoghurt, 100ml milk, 100ml pear juice (or extra milk) and a pinch each of ground cinnamon and freshly grated nutmeg. Blend until smooth. Pour into individual glasses and sprinkle a tiny pinch of cinnamon on top. If the smoothie is too thick, either dilute with a little more milk or blend in a handful of ice cubes.
2–3 SERVINGS

SCRAMBLED EGGS
AND SMOKED SALMON
ON TOASTED CROISSANTS

SERVES 4–6

4 large day-old all-butter croissants

sea salt and freshly ground black pepper

12 large eggs

50g cold unsalted butter, diced

4 tbsp double cream

1–2 tbsp snipped chives

300g smoked salmon slices

1 Trim off the ends of the croissants, then slice each one into 4 or 6 thick rounds and season lightly with salt and pepper.

2 Break the eggs into a cold heavy-based non-stick saucepan; do not season. Place the pan over a low heat and add a few knobs of butter. Using a wooden spoon, stir the eggs frequently but not constantly, just to combine the yolks and whites.

3 As the eggs start to scramble, take the pan off the heat and use a spatula to scrape the egg from the sides and base of the pan. Return to the heat and keep stirring and scraping the pan until the overall texture of the eggs is like soft curds. This should take 5–6 minutes. Don't overcook the mixture – it should be moist and soft.

4 Meanwhile, heat a dry frying pan over a medium heat and toast the croissants on each side for 1–2 minutes until golden. Place the toasted slices on individual plates.

5 When the eggs are nearing the end of cooking, take the pan off the heat, add another knob of butter and then season well. Return to the heat and stir in the cream. Once the butter has melted, remove from the heat and fold through the chives.

6 Spoon the scrambled eggs onto the toasted croissants, drape the slices of smoked salmon on top and serve immediately.

At home, Christmas lunch is always in the late afternoon because I like to do my rounds at the restaurants during lunchtime service. Everyone's first priority on Christmas morning is to open presents and then we sit down to a relaxed breakfast of scrambled eggs with smoked salmon served, indulgently, on toasted pure-butter croissants.

HAM AND POTATO CAKES

MAKES 8

500g large potatoes, such as Desirée

sea salt and freshly ground black pepper

150g cooked ham, shredded

2 tsp Dijon mustard

small handful of flat leaf parsley, leaves
   only, chopped

3 tbsp melted butter

1 egg, beaten

1 Add the whole potatoes to a pan of salted water. Bring to the boil and cook until just tender, about 20–25 minutes. Drain well and leave until cool enough to handle. Peel off the skins and, ideally, leave the potatoes uncovered in the fridge overnight.

2 Coarsely grate the potatoes into a bowl. Add a generous pinch of salt and some pepper and then mix in the ham, mustard and chopped parsley. Add 1 tbsp melted butter, then the beaten egg and mix until evenly combined.

3 Divide the mixture into 8 portions and press gently into patties. Heat half of the remaining butter in a frying pan. Add 4 potato cakes and press them gently with the back of a fish slice to flatten. Cook over a medium heat for 3–4 minutes on each side, until golden and crisp.

4 Drain the potato cakes on kitchen paper and keep warm in a low oven while you cook the rest, using the remaining butter. Serve warm.

A cross between a rösti and a hash brown, these are deliciously savoury – either eaten on their own or topped with a poached egg and a grilled tomato. They are also a great way to use up leftover ham and potatoes. For best result, use cooked potatoes that have been left uncovered – to dry out a little – in the fridge.

CINNAMON PANCAKES
WITH CARAMELISED APPLES

Pancakes:

150g self-raising flour

1½ tsp ground cinnamon

1½ tsp baking powder

pinch of fine sea salt

1½ tbsp maple syrup

225ml buttermilk

4 large eggs, separated

1–2 tbsp sunflower or groundnut oil

Caramelised apples:

3 dessert apples

2 tbsp caster sugar

1 tsp ground cinnamon

30g unsalted butter

100ml maple syrup

200ml apple juice or Calvados

To serve:

Greek yoghurt

1 To make the pancake batter, sift the flour, cinnamon, baking powder and salt into a large bowl and make a well in the middle. Add the maple syrup, buttermilk and egg yolks to the well and gradually incorporate the flour into the wet ingredients, by whisking from the middle and working outwards, until you have a fairly thick, smooth batter. In another bowl, whisk the egg whites to peaks and then fold into the batter.

2 Heat a wide non-stick frying pan over a medium heat and add 2 tsp oil. Wipe the pan with kitchen paper to oil the base evenly. Cook the pancakes in batches: drop heaped tablespoonfuls of the batter into the pan, spacing well apart and cook for 2 minutes, or until you see small bubbles rise to the surface. Flip the pancakes over and cook on the other side for 1–2 minutes, or until puffed up and golden.

3 Transfer the pancakes to a plate and keep warm in a low oven while you cook the rest, adding more oil to the pan as necessary. (You may not need to add any more after the first batch.)

4 For the caramelised apples, peel, core and cut the apples into wedges. Mix the sugar and cinnamon together and sprinkle over the apples, tossing to coat.

5 Melt the butter in the frying pan (used to cook the pancakes) and heat until starting to foam. Add the apple wedges and fry over a medium-high heat for about 5 minutes, until evenly golden brown and caramelised, turning the apples halfway.

6 Pour in the maple syrup and apple juice or Calvados and let the liquid bubble for a few minutes to make a light syrupy sauce.

7 Serve the pancakes warm, topped with the caramelised apples and syrupy pan juices, accompanied by a bowl of Greek yoghurt.

If you like American-style pancakes, then you'll love these. Light and fluffy with a hint of cinnamon, they are topped with caramelised apples in a maple syrup sauce and served with Greek yoghurt.

PROVENÇAL CHRISTMAS BREAD

MAKES 1 LARGE LOAF

500g plain flour, plus extra to dust

90g caster sugar

7g sachet active dried yeast

200ml tepid water

1½ tsp fine sea salt

finely grated zest of 1 orange

finely grated zest of 1 lemon

125ml extra virgin olive oil

1 tbsp orange flower water

1 To make the starter, put 200g of the flour into a large bowl and stir in the sugar, 1 tsp of the yeast and the water. Beat well with a wooden spoon, then cover the bowl with cling film and leave in a warm spot for at least 1½ hours, or in the fridge overnight.

2 Uncover and add the remaining flour and yeast, the salt, orange and lemon zests and the olive oil to the starter. Mix together until evenly combined.

3 Turn the slippery dough onto a lightly floured surface and knead for 5–10 minutes, until you have a soft, elastic dough. If the dough is too wet and sticky, add a little more flour. Transfer to a clean bowl, cover with cling film and leave to rise in a warm place until doubled in size, about 3–4 hours.

4 Preheat the oven to 180°C/Gas 4. Turn the dough out onto a large sheet of baking parchment and gently stretch it with your fingers to a large oval, 30–35cm long and 20–25cm wide.

5 Using a small, sharp knife, cut a 5cm long vertical slit in the dough at the top, along the middle. Make 3 further diagonal slits beneath the first slit, on both sides, to create a leaf pattern. Open the slits out with your fingers to make holes that will not close up during baking. The dough should now look like a larger leaf.

6 Lift the dough on the parchment onto a large baking sheet. Bake for 20–25 minutes until the loaf is risen and lightly golden. On removing from the oven, brush the surface with the orange flower water to soften the crust. Cool slightly before eating.

This rich, sweet olive oil bread is enjoyed over Christmas in the South of France, where it is known as pompe à l'huile. *Similar to a fougasse, with the flaky light texture of a brioche, it makes a delicious breakfast bread. As it is considered bad luck to slice the bread, it should be torn into pieces at the table. You'll need to prepare a 'starter' to get the dough going, so do plan ahead with this recipe.*

LUNCHES & SUPPERS

PUMPKIN SOUP
WITH WILD MUSHROOMS

SERVES 6

Pumpkin purée:

about 1.5kg pumpkin

sea salt and freshly ground black pepper

1 head of garlic, cut in half horizontally

handful of rosemary sprigs

olive oil, to drizzle

Soup:

1½ tbsp olive oil

1 onion, peeled and chopped

pinch of freshly grated nutmeg

30g Parmesan, freshly grated

800ml hot ham stock (see page 58)
   or chicken stock

100ml double cream

15g butter

To garnish:

1½ tbsp olive oil

400g mixed wild mushrooms
   (chanterelles, trompettes, etc.),
   cleaned and trimmed

10g butter

Parmesan shavings

1 For the pumpkin purée, preheat the oven to 170°C/Gas 3. Cut the pumpkin in half horizontally and remove the seeds – save these to make a snack (see below). Score the flesh, season with salt and pepper, then rub with the cut garlic halves. Lay rosemary sprigs and a garlic half in each pumpkin half. Drizzle with a little olive oil and place on baking trays.

2 Roast the pumpkin halves for about 1 hour until tender; the timing will depend on the variety, density and thickness. It is ready when you can effortlessly slip a knife into the thickest part of the flesh. Take out the rosemary and garlic; reserve the garlic. While still hot, scoop out the pumpkin flesh and purée in a blender or food processor.

3 For the soup, heat the olive oil in a large saucepan, add the onion and cook for 5–6 minutes until soft and translucent. Scoop out the flesh from 2 or 3 roasted garlic cloves and add to the pan with the nutmeg and a little seasoning. Sauté for 1–2 minutes.

4 Stir in the pumpkin purée and Parmesan, then pour in the stock. Bring to the boil, lower the heat and simmer for 10–12 minutes. Stir in the cream and heat for a minute.

5 In batches, ladle the soup into a blender and blend until smooth. Add the butter and blitz again to a velvety smooth texture. Pour the soup into a clean pan to reheat.

6 For the garnish, heat the olive oil in a frying pan and fry the mushrooms over a high heat for a few minutes until the moisture released has cooked off and the pan is quite dry. Add the butter, season the mushrooms and stir, then remove from the heat.

7 Pour the hot soup into warmed bowls and spoon the sautéed mushrooms into the middle. Top with Parmesan shavings, grind over some pepper and serve.

I adore this smooth, velvety soup. For a touch of luxury, I'm adding wild mushrooms – their warm, earthy flavour complements sweet, nutty pumpkin beautifully. You can use butternut squash instead of pumpkin, and chestnut mushrooms in place of wild ones if you like. For a tasty snack, wash and dry the pumpkin seeds, then roast at 190°C/Gas 5 for 10 minutes; crack and remove the husk before eating.

LINGUINE
WITH MUSHROOMS AND TRUFFLE

SERVES 4

350g dried linguine (or spaghetti)

sea salt and freshly ground black pepper

500g mixed wild mushrooms (ceps, girolles, trompettes, chanterelles, mousserons, etc.), cleaned and trimmed

1–2 tbsp olive oil

2 shallots, peeled and finely chopped

1 garlic clove, peeled and finely crushed

100ml crème fraîche

finely grated zest and juice of ½ lemon

large handful of flat leaf parsley, leaves only, chopped

drizzle of truffle oil

truffle shavings or Parmesan shavings, to finish

1 For the pasta, bring a large saucepan of well-salted water to the boil.

2 Meanwhile, tear larger mushrooms in half, leaving small ones whole. Heat the olive oil in a large frying pan and sauté the shallots and garlic for about 5 minutes, until soft and lightly golden.

3 Add the pasta to the pan of boiling salted water and cook for slightly less time than suggested on the packet.

4 Add the mushrooms to the shallots and fry over a medium heat for a few minutes. Once the mushrooms have softened and are beginning to take on a little colour, add some seasoning. Continue to fry until most of the liquid released from the mushrooms has cooked off. Stir in the crème fraîche, lemon zest and juice.

5 Drain the linguine, reserving a few tablespoonfuls of the cooking liquid. Tip the pasta onto the mushrooms and toss over a medium heat for 1–2 minutes. Add a little of the reserved cooking liquor if the sauce seems on the dry side. Add the chopped parsley and truffle oil and toss through. The pasta should now be *al dente*.

6 Divide the linguine and mushrooms among warmed plates and scatter over the truffle or Parmesan shavings to serve.

Fabulous food need not be elaborate or time-consuming, provided you use top-quality ingredients. Wild mushrooms are worth every penny as they are full of flavour. A few fresh truffle shavings add an extravagant finishing touch to this dish, but if your purse strings do not stretch that far, simply scatter over some Parmesan shavings.

IDEAS FOR SMOKED SALMON

POTTED SALMON WITH HARISSA

SERVES 4

150g unsalted butter, at room temperature
450g lightly smoked salmon fillets, skinned
2 tbsp water
2 shallots, peeled and finely chopped
1 large vine-ripened tomato, skinned, deseeded and chopped
1 garlic clove, peeled and crushed
2 tsp harissa paste
small handful of flat leaf parsley, leaves only, finely chopped
juice of ½ lemon, or to taste
sea salt and freshly ground black pepper
3 tbsp clarified (or extra unsalted) butter, melted

1 Melt 25g of the butter in a small pan, add the salmon and 2 tbsp water and cook over a low heat for 3–4 minutes, stirring often, until the fish is opaque and just cooked through. Transfer to a plate and leave to cool.

2 In the same pan, melt another 25g butter and sauté the shallots with the tomato and garlic for 8–10 minutes, until soft but not coloured. Stir in the harissa and cook for 1–2 minutes until fragrant. Take off the heat and leave to cool. Blend the mixture in a food processor with the remaining butter to a paste.

3 Flake the cooled salmon into a bowl. Add the blended butter mixture and fold through, together with the chopped parsley. Add lemon juice and seasoning to taste.

4 Spoon the mixture into ramekins. Pour over the clarified (or extra unsalted) butter to seal and store in the fridge for up to a week. Once you break into the clarified butter, eat within 2–3 days.

SMOKED SALMON CHOWDER

SERVES 4

1 tbsp olive oil
75g pancetta or streaky bacon, derinded and chopped
20g butter
1 large onion, peeled and chopped
450g floury potatoes, peeled and cut into small cubes
800ml chicken or fish stock
4 tbsp double cream
1 tbsp coarse-grain or Dijon mustard
300g smoked salmon, roughly chopped
few dill sprigs, leaves only, chopped
sea salt and freshly ground black pepper

1 Heat the olive oil in a large saucepan and gently sauté the pancetta or bacon for about 5 minutes until golden brown. Add the butter, then the onion and potatoes. Cook, stirring frequently, over a medium heat for 5–7 minutes until the onion is translucent and soft.

2 Pour in the stock and bring to the boil. Simmer, uncovered, for 12–15 minutes until the potatoes have softened. Stir in the cream and mustard. Ladle half of the soup into a blender and blitz until smooth, then return to the pan.

3 Add the smoked salmon, return to a simmer and cook, stirring, for a minute or two to warm through. Add the chopped dill and season to taste before serving.

FARFALLE WITH SMOKED SALMON AND PEAS

SERVES 4

350g farfalle (or other pasta shapes)
sea salt and freshly ground black pepper
200g frozen peas, defrosted
2 tbsp olive oil
bunch of spring onions, trimmed and sliced
100ml dry white wine or vermouth
150g crème fraîche
juice of ½ lemon
200g smoked salmon, cut into small pieces
finely grated zest of 1 lemon

1 Add the pasta to a large pan of boiling salted water and cook for slightly less than the time suggested on the packet, adding the peas for the last 2 minutes.

2 Meanwhile, heat the olive oil in a large deep frying pan. Add the spring onions and sauté gently for 2 minutes to soften slightly. Pour in the wine, bring to the boil and let bubble to reduce by half. Stir in the crème fraîche and lemon juice and simmer for about 5 minutes until thickened.

3 Drain the pasta and peas, reserving a little of the cooking water. Tip the pasta, peas and smoked salmon into the frying pan and toss well, loosening the sauce with the reserved water, if necessary. Stir over a low heat for a minute or until the pasta is *al dente* and the smoked salmon is warmed through. Stir through the lemon zest, season with pepper to taste and serve.

SMOKED SALMON AND CHAR-GRILLED POTATO SALAD

SERVES 4

600g large potatoes, such as Desirée
sea salt and freshly ground black pepper
75ml olive oil, plus extra to coat potatoes
2 small shallots, peeled and finely chopped
2 thyme sprigs, leaves only
5 juniper berries, crushed
2 tbsp cider vinegar
120g mixed salad leaves (lettuce, rocket, radicchio, etc.)
8 slices of smoked salmon

1 Add the potatoes to a pan of salted cold water, bring to the boil and cook for 15–20 minutes until just tender. Drain well and peel off the skins once the potatoes are cool enough to handle.

2 Heat the olive oil in a small pan and add the shallots, thyme leaves, crushed juniper and some salt and pepper. Cook over a low heat for 10–15 minutes, until the shallots are soft and pale golden. Take off the heat, stir in the cider vinegar and check the seasoning.

3 Heat a large griddle pan. Slice the potatoes into 5mm rounds and toss with a little olive oil and some seasoning. Cook in the griddle pan for 3–4 minutes on each side, until golden and char-grilled.

4 Toss the salad leaves in enough of the shallot dressing to coat and then divide among serving plates, piling it into a tidy mound in the centre. Arrange the char-grilled potatoes around the salad and drape the smoked salmon slices on top. Drizzle the smoked salmon with some of the remaining dressing and serve.

POACHED SIDE OF SALMON
WITH A LIGHT TARRAGON MAYONNAISE

SERVES 4

700g side of salmon (or larger, see below)

trimmings from 2 fennel tops

trimmings from 1 head of celery

1 small onion, peeled and sliced

large pinch of sea salt

150ml white wine

splash of tarragon vinegar

2 star anise

few white peppercorns, crushed

small handful of flat leaf parsley

2 bay leaves

1 lemon, sliced

Tarragon mayonnaise:

1 large egg yolk

1 tsp English mustard

1 tbsp tarragon white wine vinegar

300ml sunflower oil

squeeze of lemon juice

splash of water

1 tbsp chopped tarragon leaves

finely grated zest of 1 lemon

sea salt and freshly ground black pepper

1 Half-fill a roasting tray (or a pan large enough to fit the salmon) with water. Put all the ingredients except the salmon in the pan. Bring to the boil, then reduce the heat to a gentle simmer. Lower the side of salmon into the tray, skin side down, and spoon some of the vegetables and lemon slices on top. If necessary, top up with more water to cover the fish. Simmer very gently for 4 minutes (allow an extra minute for a larger side). Turn the heat off and leave the salmon to cool in the poaching liquor.

2 To make the tarragon mayonnaise, put the egg yolk, mustard and tarragon vinegar into a bowl and wrap a tea-towel around the base of the bowl to steady it as you whisk. Start whisking and continue until the egg yolk mixture becomes very thick and pale; do not season at this stage. Gradually whisk in the oil, a little drizzle at a time, until it is all incorporated and you have a thick, emulsified mayonnaise base. Stir in the lemon juice and loosen the mayonnaise with a splash of water. Stir in the chopped tarragon and lemon zest and season with salt and pepper to taste.

3 Once the salmon has cooled, carefully lift it out using two fish slices and place on a large board. Gently peel off the skin and check the fish for pin bones, removing any you find with tweezers.

4 Divide the salmon into portions and serve with the tarragon mayonnaise and a leafy salad on the side.

I often cook salmon over the festive holiday period – if we've had a succession of poultry and meat it makes a pleasant change. I'll usually poach a large side – around 1kg – so there is enough to make my salmon salad niçoise (see page 106) for lunch the following day.

SALMON SALAD NIÇOISE
WITH CODDLED EGGS

SERVES 4–6

200g cherry tomatoes

sea salt and freshly ground black pepper

bunch of large basil leaves, shredded

finely grated zest of 1 lemon

2–3 tbsp olive oil, plus extra to drizzle

400g new potatoes, halved

200g green beans

3–4 heads of baby gem lettuce, washed
   and trimmed

6–8 tbsp tarragon mayonnaise
   (see page 105)

100g pitted black olives

300–400g cold poached salmon
   (see page 105)

Coddled eggs:

softened butter, to grease

4–6 basil leaves

4–6 anchovy fillets

4–6 medium eggs, at room temperature

1 Preheat the oven to 180°C/Gas 4 (for the coddled eggs). Slice the cherry tomatoes in half, place in a bowl and season with salt and pepper. Top with the basil leaves, lemon zest and a little drizzle of olive oil. Stir together and set aside to marinate.

2 Add the potatoes to a pan of boiling salted water and cook for 12–15 minutes, or until just tender; remove with a slotted spoon and set aside. Add the green beans to the boiling water and blanch for a minute, then drain.

3 For the coddled eggs, generously butter 4–6 espresso cups or small ramekins and sprinkle with salt and pepper. Lay a basil leaf and an anchovy fillet in the base of each cup or ramekin, then crack an egg in. Stand them in a deep baking tray and surround with enough boiling water to come three-quarters of the way up the sides. Carefully transfer to the oven and cook for 6–8 minutes, or until the whites are set but the yolks are still creamy.

4 Meanwhile, heat a wide frying pan until it is very hot and then add 2 tbsp olive oil. Add the potatoes, cut side down, and swirl the oil around them. Once the potatoes are golden brown on the flat side, turn them over and add the blanched green beans. Season with salt and pepper and cook, tossing the vegetables, for a further 30 seconds, then take off the heat.

5 To assemble the salad, tear the outer leaves from the lettuce hearts and arrange on a platter or individual plates. Cut the hearts into wedges and dip the leafy ends in tarragon mayonnaise. Arrange on the platter (or plates) with the sautéed potatoes, green beans, marinated tomatoes and olives.

6 Run a knife around the coddled eggs, then lift them out and place on the salad. Break the poached salmon into large flakes and arrange on top. Drizzle over a little more tarragon mayonnaise and grind over some pepper. Serve at once, with the rest of the mayonnaise in a bowl on the side.

This salad niçoise with a twist – featuring fresh, poached salmon instead of tinned tuna, coddled eggs and a light tarragon mayonnaise – is special enough for any celebratory meal.

IDEAS FOR COOKED TURKEY

SOBA NOODLES AND TURKEY IN MISO BROTH

SERVES 4

300–400g cooked turkey, sliced
1 large garlic clove, peeled and crushed
2 tbsp light soy sauce
1 tbsp sesame oil, plus extra to drizzle
sea salt and freshly ground black pepper
2 litres chicken or turkey stock
5cm knob of fresh root ginger, peeled and sliced
1 piece of kombu
2 tsp caster sugar
3–4 tbsp dark soy sauce, or to taste
3 tbsp miso paste
350g dried buckwheat soba noodles
150g shiitake mushrooms, trimmed and thinly sliced
3–4 spring onions (green part only), thinly sliced on the diagonal,
   to garnish

1 Toss the turkey in a bowl with the garlic, soy sauce, sesame oil and some pepper. Cover and set aside.
2 Pour the stock into a large saucepan and add the ginger, kombu, sugar and soy sauce. Bring to the boil, lower the heat and simmer for about 20 minutes. Fish out and discard the ginger slices and kombu, then add the miso and stir until dissolved.
3 Meanwhile, cook the noodles in a large pan of boiling salted water according to the packet instructions, until tender but retaining a bite.
4 Add the mushrooms to the miso broth and simmer for a few minutes, then add the turkey and simmer for another 1½–2 minutes.
5 Drain the noodles in a colander and toss with a little sesame oil. Divide among warmed bowls and ladle the soup on top, dividing the turkey and vegetables equally. Garnish with spring onions and serve.

TURKEY, CRANBERRY AND WILD RICE PILAF

SERVES 4–6

25g butter
1 large onion, peeled and chopped
300g mixed basmati and wild rice
½ tsp ground ginger
1 cinnamon stick
75g dried cranberries
750ml hot chicken or turkey stock
300g cooked turkey, shredded or thinly sliced
sea salt and freshly ground black pepper
handful of flat leaf parsley leaves, chopped
handful of nuts, toasted and chopped

1 Melt the butter in a heavy-based medium saucepan. Add the onion and fry until soft and pale golden, about 8–10 minutes. Meanwhile, rinse the rice in a sieve under cold running water. Tip the rice into the pan and stir the grains to lightly toast them for 2 minutes.
2 Add the ginger, cinnamon stick and dried cranberries. Pour in the hot stock and stir in the turkey with some seasoning. Bring to the boil, stirring, then lower the heat. Lay a crumpled, dampened piece of greaseproof paper on the surface and put a lid on the pan. Turn the heat right down and cook for about 10 minutes until most of the stock has been absorbed. Turn off the heat and leave to stand, covered, for 10 minutes.
3 Remove the lid and paper and fluff up the rice with a fork. Scatter over the parsley and toasted nuts and serve.

TURKEY CURRY

SERVES 4–6

2 onions, peeled and roughly chopped
5cm knob of fresh root ginger, peeled and roughly chopped
4 garlic cloves, peeled and roughly chopped
2 large red chillies, deseeded and roughly chopped
4 tbsp vegetable or sunflower oil
1 tsp ground coriander
1 tsp ground cumin
1 tsp garam masala
1 cinnamon stick
400g tin chopped tomatoes
200ml coconut milk
2 tsp soft brown sugar
500ml chicken or turkey stock
sea salt and freshly ground black pepper
about 400g cooked turkey
handful of coriander leaves

1 Blitz the onions, ginger, garlic and chillies in a blender with a splash of water to a paste. Heat the oil in a large pan, add the paste and fry over a medium-low heat until it starts to take on some colour, about 10 minutes. Add all the spices, stir and cook for another couple of minutes until fragrant.
2 Add the chopped tomatoes, coconut milk, sugar and stock. Season with salt and pepper to taste and give everything a good stir. Simmer for about 30 minutes, stirring occasionally.
3 Add the turkey and bring to a simmer. Lower the heat and simmer gently for another 5 minutes. Scatter over the coriander leaves and serve with steamed basmati rice.

TURKEY, CHORIZO AND BEAN STEW

SERVES 4

1 tbsp olive oil
1 onion, peeled and chopped
150g cooking chorizo sausage, peeled and cut into chunks
400g can peeled plum tomatoes, broken up with a fork
1 tbsp tomato purée
175ml red wine
2 thyme sprigs, leaves only, finely chopped
2 rosemary sprigs, leaves only, finely chopped
sea salt and freshly ground black pepper
200g cooked turkey
400g tin cannellini beans, drained and rinsed
large handful of shredded Savoy cabbage
500ml boiling chicken stock
freshly grated Parmesan, to serve

1 Heat the olive oil in a pan, add the onion and sauté for 5–6 minutes until soft and lightly golden. Add the chorizo and fry for a few minutes until it starts to release its oil. Stir in the crushed plum tomatoes, tomato purée, red wine, herbs and some seasoning. Bring to the boil, lower the heat and simmer for 10 minutes.
2 Meanwhile, cut or shred the cooked turkey into large pieces. Add to the pan, along with the cannellini beans, cabbage and stock. Return to the boil and cook over a medium heat for 7–10 minutes, until the cabbage is cooked and the sauce has thickened. Taste for seasoning.
3 Serve topped with a sprinkling of Parmesan and with plenty of crusty bread on the side.

PAN-FRIED DUCK BREAST
WITH SPICED ORANGE
AND CRANBERRY SAUCE

SERVES 4

4 duck breasts, about 225g each

4 juniper berries

pinch of caraway seeds

1 tsp allspice

sea salt and freshly ground black pepper

Spiced orange and cranberry sauce:

100ml ruby port

100g fresh cranberries

finely grated zest and juice of 1 orange

½ cinnamon stick

1 star anise

300ml chicken stock

1–2 tsp cranberry or redcurrant jelly, to taste

30g butter, diced

1 Lightly score the skins of the duck breasts with a sharp knife. Using a pestle and mortar, grind the juniper berries, caraway seeds, allspice, 1 tsp salt and a few grinds of pepper to a powder. Rub the spice mix all over the duck breasts and leave to stand for about 10 minutes.

2 Lay the duck breasts, skin side down, in a dry heavy-based large frying pan and gradually turn up the heat. Fry for 5–10 minutes, until most of the fat has rendered and the skin is golden brown.

3 Turn the duck breasts over and lightly brown the other side for a couple of minutes, or until they feel slightly springy when pressed. Remove from the pan and leave to rest in a warm place while you make the sauce.

4 For the sauce, pour off excess fat from the frying pan and place over a high heat. Pour in the port, stirring to deglaze, and let bubble for a minute. Add the remaining ingredients, except the butter, and bring to the boil. Let bubble until the liquid has reduced by two-thirds and thickened to a syrupy consistency. The cranberries should be very soft; squash a few with a wooden spoon, leaving the others whole. Add any juices from the resting duck. Taste and adjust the seasoning and add a little more jelly if desired. Finally, add the butter and shake the pan to incorporate it as it melts.

5 Slice the duck breasts on the diagonal and fan them out on warmed serving plates. Spoon the sauce around the duck and serve with parsnip purée and creamed cabbage with thyme (see page 61) if you like.

This is an elegant main course, perfect for a dinner party over the festive period. I would recommend buying either Gressingham or Barbary duck breasts – both breeds are prized for their superlative flavour. For convenience, the sauce can be made in advance and reheated just before serving.

SHALLOT TART TATIN
WITH ROASTED TOMATOES AND GOAT'S CHEESE

SERVES 4

2 large vine-ripened tomatoes

3 tbsp olive oil

sea salt and freshly ground black pepper

1 thyme sprig, leaves only, plus extra
  to garnish

50g caster sugar, plus 1 tbsp

75g unsalted butter, cut into cubes

3 tbsp balsamic vinegar

300g large shallots

150ml chicken or vegetable stock

300g puff pastry

plain flour, to dust

120g goat's cheese (such as Dorstone,
  Rosary or Pant-Ysgawn), crumbled

1 Preheat the oven to 180°C/Gas 4. Halve the tomatoes lengthways and place, cut side up, in a small shallow roasting tin. Trickle over 2 tbsp olive oil, season with a little salt and pepper and sprinkle over the thyme leaves. Roast for about 20 minutes, until the tomatoes have softened a little, but are still holding their shape. Set aside to cool.

2 Meanwhile, for the caramel, sprinkle the 50g sugar into a 20cm ovenproof frying pan and place over a medium heat, tilting the pan as the sugar begins to melt. As soon as the caramel turns a terracotta brown colour, take off the heat and stir in 50g butter and the balsamic vinegar (protect your hand with a cloth as the hot caramel is likely to splutter). If it hardens, stir over a medium-low heat until it melts again. Leave to cool.

3 Blanch the shallots in their skins in boiling water for 30 seconds. Drain, refresh under cold running water, then peel and trim the root ends. Halve the shallots lengthways.

4 Heat the remaining oil and butter in a large frying pan. Add the shallots with 1 tbsp sugar and sauté over a medium heat for 10 minutes until golden brown all over. Pour in the stock, bring to the boil and braise for 10 minutes, or until the shallots are tender and most of the liquid has cooked off. Using a slotted spoon, transfer the shallots to the cooled caramel, leaving behind any syrupy liquid. Leave to cool.

5 Roll out the pastry on a lightly floured surface to the thickness of a £1 coin and cut out a 23cm round, using a plate as a guide. Use the rolling pin to lift the pastry over the shallots in the pan, positioning it centrally. Tuck the edges down the side of the pan, enclosing the shallots. Refrigerate for 1–2 hours, or overnight if making in advance.

6 Preheat the oven to 200°C/Gas 6. Bake the tart for 30–35 minutes, or until the pastry is golden brown. Let stand for 5 minutes; meanwhile, warm the tomatoes in the oven.

7 Invert the tatin onto a large plate. Arrange the tomatoes and goat's cheese on top, then drizzle over any tomato juices from the roasting tin. Garnish with thyme to serve.

An impressive dish that could be served as a main course for a vegetarian Christmas dinner. All the prep is done ahead – just pop the tart into the oven straight from the fridge as you serve the starter.

IDEAS FOR COOKED HAM

PEA AND HAM SOUP WITH MINTED CRÈME FRAÎCHE

SERVES 4

1 litre leftover ham stock (see page 58)
1kg frozen peas, defrosted
squeeze of lemon juice
sea salt and freshly ground black pepper
100g cooked ham, shredded or cubed
100g crème fraîche
handful of mint leaves, shredded

1 Bring the ham stock to the boil in a large saucepan. Tip in the peas, return to the boil and simmer for about 3 minutes, until just tender and still bright green. Drain, reserving the stock.
2 Blitz the peas in a blender with enough of the stock to achieve a smooth, velvety texture. Return to the pan and add the lemon juice and salt and pepper to taste. Stir in the ham.
3 For the minted crème fraîche, simply mix the crème fraîche and mint together in a bowl and season with a little salt and pepper.
4 Reheat the soup if necessary and then ladle into warmed bowls. Top each portion with a dollop of the minted crème fraîche; hand the rest around separately.

SPAGHETTI 'CARBONARA'

SERVES 4

350g dried spaghetti
sea salt and freshly ground black pepper
2 tbsp olive oil
2 garlic cloves, peeled and crushed
200g cooked ham, shredded
2 large egg yolks
150ml double cream
1–2 tbsp wholegrain mustard
100g Parmesan, freshly grated

1 Add the spaghetti to a large saucepan of boiling salted water and cook for slightly less than the time suggested on the packet.
2 Meanwhile, heat the olive oil in a large frying pan with the garlic and ham and sauté for 2–3 minutes to infuse the oil with the flavour of garlic and warm the ham through.
3 In a bowl, whisk the egg yolks with the cream, mustard, half the Parmesan and some seasoning.
4 Drain the pasta as soon as it is ready, reserving some of the cooking water. Discard the garlic, then tip the spaghetti into the frying pan, followed by the egg and cream mix. Briefly toss over a low heat to coat the pasta in the creamy sauce, adding some of the reserved liquid if the sauce seems a little thick, then take off the heat.
5 Serve the pasta on warmed plates, sprinkled with the remaining Parmesan and some pepper.

GLAZED HAM SALAD WITH ROQUEFORT DRESSING

SERVES 4
3 large eggs
200g baby plum or cherry tomatoes
1 head of Romaine lettuce, trimmed
250g cooked ham
2 ripe medium avocados

Dressing:
4 tbsp extra virgin olive oil
1½ tbsp red wine vinegar
2 tsp Dijon mustard
sea salt and freshly ground black pepper
75g Roquefort cheese, crumbled
2 tsp chopped chives

1 Put the eggs in a small saucepan, add enough cold water to cover by about 2cm and bring to the boil, then lower the heat and simmer gently for 6 minutes. Drain and cool under cold running water, then shell and cut into quarters.
2 To make the dressing, in a bowl, whisk together the olive oil, wine vinegar and mustard with a pinch each of salt and pepper. Stir in the Roquefort and chives and set aside.
3 Quarter the tomatoes, shred the lettuce and chop the ham. Halve, stone and peel the avocados, then cut into chunks. Arrange the salad ingredients, including the egg wedges, on individual plates and drizzle over the Roquefort dressing to serve.

LEEK, HAM AND MUSHROOM PIES

SERVES 4
15g butter
4 leeks (white part only), trimmed and sliced
sea salt and freshly ground black pepper
300g chestnut mushrooms, cleaned and sliced
splash of dry white wine
150ml double cream
150ml leftover ham stock (see page 58) or chicken stock
1 tsp Dijon or coarse-grain mustard
200g cooked ham, cubed
300g ready-made puff pastry
plain flour, to dust
2 medium egg yolks, beaten with 1 tbsp water (eggwash)

1 Melt the butter in a wide pan and add the leeks with some seasoning. Fry for a few minutes, then add the mushrooms and cook over a high heat for 4–5 minutes until the moisture released has cooked off. Add the wine and reduce right down. Add the cream and stock and bubble until reduced by one-third or until thickened. Add the mustard and seasoning to taste. Take off the heat and stir in the ham.
2 Divide the filling among 4 individual pie dishes and set aside to cool completely. Preheat the oven to 190°C/Gas 5.
3 Roll out the pastry on a lightly floured surface to the thickness of a £1 coin. Cut out 4 neat rounds, slightly larger than the pie dishes. Brush the rims of the dishes with water. Cut strips from the remaining pastry and position on the wetted rims. Drape the pastry lids on top and press the edges onto the rims to seal. Crimp the pastry edges and cut a small steam hole in each lid with the tip of a knife.
4 Brush the pastry with eggwash and bake the pies for 20–25 minutes, until the pastry is golden brown and the filling is piping hot.

WINTER MINESTRONE
WITH WALNUT PESTO

SERVES 4

2 tbsp olive oil

knob of butter

2 carrots, peeled and diced

2 parsnips, peeled and diced

1 swede or 2 turnips, peeled and diced

2 celery sticks, trimmed and diced

1 fennel bulb, trimmed and diced

1 potato, peeled and diced

2 thyme sprigs, leaves only

1 garlic clove, peeled and crushed

850ml leftover ham stock (see page 58),
   or chicken stock

sea salt and freshly ground black pepper

150g diced ham (optional)

Walnut pesto:

small bunch of flat leaf parsley

85g walnut halves

60g Parmesan, freshly grated

1 garlic clove, peeled and chopped

1 tbsp chopped sage

120ml olive oil

squeeze of lemon juice, to taste

1 Heat the olive oil and butter in a heavy-based saucepan. Add all of the vegetables, except the potato, and sweat for about 10 minutes, stirring frequently over a medium heat. Stir in the potato, thyme and garlic and sauté for a few minutes.

2 Pour in enough stock to cover the vegetables and bring to the boil. Lower the heat to a simmer. Season well with salt and pepper and cook for another 15–20 minutes until the vegetables are soft.

3 Meanwhile, make the pesto. Tear the parsley leaves from their stalks and put them into a small food processor with the walnuts, Parmesan, garlic and sage. Pulse a few times, then with the motor running, start to drizzle in the olive oil and blend until you have a pesto-like consistency. Add lemon juice, salt and pepper to taste. (If not serving immediately, transfer the pesto to a small clean jar, cover with a film of olive oil, seal and refrigerate.)

4 Just before you are ready to serve the soup, add the diced ham, if using, and reheat gently for a few minutes. Adjust the seasoning to taste, then ladle into warmed soup plates. Hand round a bowl of walnut pesto for guests to spoon onto their soup.

This makes fantastic use of any leftover stock (and meat) from a glazed ham. It's a real celebration of hardy winter root vegetables – which can be varied according to what you have to hand – and the rustic walnut pesto is a lovely enhancement. You can also bulk up the soup by adding a generous handful of macaroni or similar pasta. Spread any extra pesto on toasted ciabatta slices and serve on the side.

PUMPKIN RISOTTO

SERVES 4

300g risotto rice, such as Arborio,
Vialone Nano or Carnaroli

1.3 litres vegetable or chicken stock

2 tbsp olive oil

1 large onion, peeled and finely chopped

sea salt and freshly ground black pepper

400g pumpkin purée (see page 99)

few knobs of butter

2 tbsp mascarpone

3 tbsp freshly grated Parmesan, plus
shavings, to serve

1 Rinse the rice in a sieve under cold running water and drain well. Bring the stock to the boil in a medium saucepan, then add the rice. Lower the heat slightly and simmer for 7 minutes – until almost but not quite *al dente*. Drain immediately, reserving the stock, and spread the rice on a tray to cool. Refrigerate until needed.

2 About 10–15 minutes before you are ready to serve, heat the olive oil in a medium saucepan. Add the onion with some seasoning and sauté over a medium-low heat for 5 minutes, or until softened and translucent but not browned. Stir in the pumpkin purée and cook for another 5 minutes. Meanwhile, bring the reserved stock to the boil in another saucepan.

3 Add the pre-cooked rice to the onion and pumpkin, then add just enough hot stock to cover the rice. Quickly bring to a simmer and cook for a few minutes. Taste the rice to see if it is *al dente*. If not, add a little more stock and cook for a few more minutes.

4 Check the seasoning and stir in the butter, followed by the mascarpone and grated Parmesan. Spoon the risotto onto warmed serving plates, scatter over some Parmesan shavings and serve.

I had to include a risotto in this book, if only because it's a diversion from all the festive meat and poultry. I made it with leftover purée from my pumpkin soup, but you can certainly use fresh, diced squash or pumpkin – just sauté with some butter and seasoning until tender, then stir into the cooked risotto before serving. This is the way we cook risotto at the restaurants – parboiling the rice first so that you only need about 10 minutes to finish off the dish before serving.

BUBBLE AND SQUEAK CAKES

MAKES 10–12

1kg floury potatoes, such as King Edward
   or Maris Piper, peeled and quartered

sea salt and freshly ground black pepper

500g cooked Brussels sprouts

40g butter

50g plain flour

olive oil, to shallow-fry

1 Add the potatoes to a saucepan of salted water, bring to the boil and cook for 15–20 minutes until tender. Meanwhile, finely shred the cooked Brussels sprouts.

2 Drain the potatoes and push them through a potato ricer, or mash thoroughly using a potato masher. Return to the pan and stir over a low heat for 1–2 minutes to dry them out. Add the butter to melt and mix well, then take off the heat.

3 While the potatoes are still warm, mix in the shredded Brussels sprouts. Season well with salt and pepper to taste. Tip the flour onto a plate and season with a pinch each of salt and pepper. Shape the potato and sprout mixture into 10–12 patties and lightly coat with the seasoned flour.

4 Heat a 5mm depth of olive oil in a large frying pan. In batches, shallow-fry the savoury cakes for 2 minutes on each side or until golden and crisp. Drain on kitchen paper and sprinkle with a little salt. Serve at once, on warmed plates.

This is a brilliant way to use up leftover Brussels sprouts, or you can cook them from scratch – it takes only an extra 3 minutes to parboil or steam them. Alternatively, you can make the bubble and squeak using cooked, shredded Savoy cabbage and spring onions. Eat them on their own, or topped with a fried or poached egg and a couple of crispy bacon rashers.

IDEAS FOR STILTON

STILTON AND WALNUT PALMIERS

MAKES 24
250g ready-made puff pastry
plain flour, to dust
125g Stilton
40g walnuts, finely chopped
1 tsp thyme leaves

1 Roll out the pastry on a lightly floured surface to a rectangle, about 30 x 40cm. Trim the edges to neaten with a sharp knife. Position the pastry with a long edge closest to you.
2 Crumble the Stilton as finely as you can over the pastry, then scatter over the walnuts and thyme leaves. Roll the pastry from both long ends to the middle, to make two spirals that meet in the middle.
3 Lift onto a baking sheet and freeze for 30 minutes, or until firm. (If you freeze it for longer, let it thaw at room temperature for 15 minutes before slicing.)
4 Preheat the oven to 190°C/Gas 5. Cut the joined rolls across into 1cm thick slices and arrange on a large baking tray, spacing well apart. Bake for 15–20 minutes until golden brown and crisp. Carefully transfer to a wire rack to cool. Store in an airtight container unless serving straightaway.

CELERIAC, APPLE AND STILTON SOUP

SERVES 6
knob of butter
1 tbsp olive oil
1 onion, peeled and chopped
700g celeriac
350g potatoes
sea salt and freshly ground black pepper
handful of thyme sprigs, leaves only
1.2 litres vegetable stock
2 dessert apples, peeled, cored and diced
squeeze of lemon juice
50ml double cream
150g Stilton, crumbled

1 Melt the butter with the olive oil in a large saucepan, add the onion and fry gently for 5–6 minutes until softened. Meanwhile, peel the celeriac and potatoes and cut into chunks, then add to the pan with some seasoning and thyme. Stir well.
2 Pour in the stock and bring to the boil, then lower the heat and simmer for 20 minutes. Add the apples and lemon juice and cook for a further 5–10 minutes until the vegetables and apples are very soft.
3 Whiz the soup in a blender or using a hand-held stick blender until smooth. Return to the pan and stir in the cream, adding a splash of boiling water if the soup is a little thick.
4 Reheat gently, then add half the Stilton and stir until melted. Taste and adjust the seasoning if necessary. Pour the soup into warmed bowls and scatter the remaining Stilton on top to serve.

GRIDDLED FIG SALAD WITH STILTON DRESSING

SERVES 4
6 ripe firm figs
1 tbsp olive oil
sea salt and freshly ground black pepper
120g mixed salad leaves (rocket, oak leaf lettuce, red chard, etc.)
50g pecan nut halves, toasted
50g Stilton

Stilton dressing:
50g Stilton, crumbled
3 tbsp crème fraîche
1–2 tsp honey
1 small garlic clove, peeled and finely crushed
1 tbsp sherry vinegar
3 tbsp boiling water

1 For the dressing, put the Stilton, crème fraîche, honey, garlic, sherry vinegar and water into a small food processor and blend until smooth. Season with a little salt if needed and pepper to taste.
2 Heat up a griddle. Cut the figs in half and rub with a little olive oil and a pinch each of salt and pepper. Cook on the hot griddle for 2–3 minutes on each side, until slightly softened and lightly char-grilled. Remove from the heat.
3 Put the salad leaves in a bowl, drizzle with some of the dressing and toss lightly. Pile into the centre of four serving plates. Arrange the griddled figs around the outside and scatter the toasted pecans in between them. Drizzle the figs and pecans with some more dressing and crumble the Stilton on top. Serve with crusty bread on the side.

STEAK WITH MUSHROOM AND BLUE CHEESE SAUCE

SERVES 4
4 sirloin or rib-eye steaks, about 200–250g each
sea salt and freshly ground black pepper
1 tbsp olive oil
knob of butter

Mushroom and blue cheese sauce:
2 tbsp olive oil
200g chestnut mushrooms, cleaned and sliced
1 garlic clove, peeled and crushed
1 thyme sprig, leaves only
150ml dry sherry
1 tbsp sherry vinegar or balsamic vinegar
150ml good-quality beef stock
2 tbsp crème fraîche
50g Stilton, crumbled
handful of flat leaf parsley, leaves only, chopped

1 To make the sauce, heat the olive oil in a large frying pan and sauté the mushrooms, garlic and thyme for 5 minutes until soft. Pour in the sherry, bring to the boil and reduce to a syrupy glaze. Splash in the vinegar and cook until reduced right down. Stir in the stock, bring to the boil, then simmer for about 5 minutes, or until reduced by half.
2 Season the steaks well. Heat the olive oil in a large frying pan, add the steaks and cook for 1½–2½ minutes on each side, adding the butter halfway through and basting the steaks as they cook. Once cooked to your liking, transfer to a warmed plate and rest for 5 minutes.
3 Meanwhile, add the crème fraîche and Stilton to the sauce and stir until the cheese has melted. Check the seasoning and add the chopped parsley and any juices from the rested beef. Serve with the steaks.

SWEET TREATS

ITALIAN-STYLE TRIFLE

SERVES 8

Marsala jelly:

2 medium sheets leaf gelatine
(11 x 7.5cm)

200ml Marsala

2 tbsp caster sugar

Trifle:

500g mascarpone

6 tbsp icing sugar, plus extra to finish

finely grated zest of 2 oranges

5–6 tbsp Vin Santo or Marsala,
plus extra to drizzle

50g chopped mixed peel (optional)

300ml double cream

about 250g panettone

dark chocolate, for grating

1 To make the jelly, soak the gelatine sheets in a shallow dish of cold water. Meanwhile, put the Marsala and sugar into a small saucepan and stir over a low heat until the sugar has dissolved. Bring almost to the boil and then take off the heat. Squeeze the gelatine to remove excess water, then add to the Marsala syrup and stir until fully dissolved. Pour the mixture into a shallow container and leave to cool, then cover and refrigerate for a few hours until set.

2 Put the mascarpone into a bowl and sift in the icing sugar. Add the orange zest, Vin Santo or Marsala and mixed peel, if using. Beat until evenly mixed.

3 In a separate bowl, whisk the cream to soft peaks and then fold into the mascarpone mixture, using a large metal spoon or spatula.

4 Cut the panettone into small cubes and place in a bowl. Drizzle over a little Vin Santo or Marsala and toss to coat.

5 To assemble the trifle, place a layer of panettone in a large glass serving bowl. Roughly chop the Marsala jelly and scatter half over the panettone layer. Spread half the mascarpone mixture on top. Repeat these layers, then chill until ready to serve.

6 To finish, grate a layer of chocolate over the surface.

Featuring Italian ingredients, this is most definitely a boozy trifle – one you can prepare ahead and leave in the fridge to allow the flavours to mingle. If you like fruit in your trifle, add peeled, diced pears or orange segments in between the layers. For a sophisticated presentation, assemble individual trifles in Martini glasses.

CHRISTMAS BOMBE

SERVES 8–10

400g good-quality chocolate Swiss roll (jumbo size)

390g jar cherries in kirsch-flavoured syrup

180g caster sugar

75ml water

2 large egg whites

300ml double cream

50g preserved stem ginger in syrup, chopped, plus 1 tbsp syrup from the jar

1 tbsp Grand Marnier or Cointreau

50g chopped mixed glacé fruit

30g marron glacé (optional), chopped

30g shelled pistachio nuts, toasted and roughly chopped

few redcurrant sprigs, to finish (optional)

icing sugar, to dust (optional)

1 Line a 2-litre bowl with a double layer of cling film, leaving some excess overhanging the rim. Cut the Swiss roll into 1cm slices and use to line the base and sides of the bowl, cutting a few of the slices into pieces to fill the gaps as necessary. Drain the cherries, reserving the syrup. Drizzle the Swiss roll slices with the kirsch syrup, saving a few tablespoonfuls for the top. Set aside.

2 Put the sugar and water into a small heavy-based saucepan and stir over a low heat to dissolve. Increase the heat to high and boil until the syrup registers 120°C on a sugar thermometer. Meanwhile, in a clean large bowl, whisk the egg whites to stiff peaks.

3 When the sugar syrup is ready, gradually pour onto the egg whites in a steady stream, whisking as you do so. Continue to whisk until the meringue has doubled in volume and the sides of the bowl no longer feels hot.

4 In another bowl, whisk the cream to soft peaks. Fold in the ginger syrup and orange liqueur, followed by the meringue. Taste and sweeten with a little more ginger syrup if required. Stir through the cherries, chopped ginger, glacé fruit, marron glacé, if using, and chopped pistachios. Spoon into the Swiss roll-lined bowl and level the top.

5 Cover with the remaining Swiss roll slices, cutting them to fit as necessary. Drizzle with the rest of the kirsch syrup, then fold the excess cling film over the top to seal.

6 Place a flat plate on top (one that just fits inside the rim) and weigh it down with a heavy tin. Chill for an hour, then remove the weight, wrap and freeze the bombe.

7 To serve, unwrap the bombe and place on a flat plate or cake stand. Decorate with sprigs of redcurrants dusted with icing sugar if you like, or serve it just as it is. Let stand at room temperature for about 15 minutes before slicing.

With a surprise frozen creamy filling dotted with sweet festive ingredients, this is a great dessert for Christmas. It looks impressive and, best of all, it can be made well in advance and kept in the freezer for up to a month. For a speedy cheat's version, you could replace my creamy meringue filling with good-quality ready-made ice cream.

PEAR AND AMARETTO CHEESECAKE

SERVES 8–10

Poached pears:

2 large pears

50g caster sugar

100ml water

1 vanilla pod

Base:

150g digestive biscuits

50g unsalted butter

2 tbsp chocolate spread, such as Nutella

Filling:

300g full-fat cream cheese (i.e. Philadelphia-type)

125g caster sugar

550ml double cream

3 tbsp amaretto liqueur

100g amaretti biscuits, lightly crushed

To decorate:

120g good-quality dark chocolate

icing sugar, to dust

1 First, poach the pears for the filling. Peel, quarter and core the pears, then cut into 1cm dice. Dissolve the sugar in the water in a small saucepan over a low heat. Split the vanilla pod and scrape out the seeds into a large bowl; set aside for later. Add the pod to the sugar syrup and simmer for a few minutes to infuse. Add the diced pears and poach gently for about 3 minutes. Drain and leave to cool.

2 For the cheesecake base, blitz the digestives in a food processor to fine crumbs, then tip into a bowl. Melt the butter in a small pan and stir in the chocolate spread. Add to the biscuit crumbs and mix well. Spread the mixture evenly over the base of a 23–24cm springform cake tin, pressing down lightly. Chill for at least 20 minutes until set.

3 For the filling, add the cream cheese and sugar to the vanilla seeds. Using a hand whisk, beat the mixture until well blended. Add 450ml of the cream and the liqueur and whisk to soft peaks. Fold in the crushed amaretti biscuits and poached pears.

4 Spoon the filling on top of the biscuit base and level the surface. Chill for at least 30 minutes, or until firm. Spread over the remaining cream to form a thin layer, then chill again.

5 For the decoration, melt the chocolate in a heatproof bowl over a pan of hot water, then spread in an even layer on a marble slab or the underside of a clean baking sheet. Leave until just set, then draw a sharp knife across the surface at an angle of about 25° to shave off large curls.

6 To unmould the cheesecake, run a hot thin-bladed knife around the edge and remove the side of the tin. Slide a palette knife under the cheesecake and transfer to a flat plate. Arrange the chocolate curls decoratively on top, then dust with icing sugar. Cut into slices to serve. (This dessert will keep in the fridge for a day or two.)

Simple and delicious, this cheesecake requires neither gelatine nor baking. To save time, you can use a tin of pear quarters in natural juice, but freshly poached pears lend a better flavour and texture.

VANILLA SHORTBREAD

SERVES 8

1 vanilla pod

2 medium eggs

125g unsalted butter, at room
temperature

90g caster sugar (or vanilla sugar),
plus extra to sprinkle

250g plain flour, plus extra to dust

small pinch of sea salt

1 Split the vanilla pod in half lengthways and scrape out the seeds with the tip of the knife into a bowl. Add the eggs and beat lightly.

2 Beat the butter and sugar together using an electric mixer until smooth and creamy. Gradually work in the beaten eggs, a little at a time. Sift the flour and salt together and slowly add to the mixer. Beat on low speed until all the flour is incorporated; stop as soon as the dough comes together.

3 Tip the dough out onto a lightly floured surface and, using floured hands, press together gently to form a ball. (Don't knead the dough or it will become tough.) Flatten the ball and lightly roll out to a 1cm thick round. Using a 20cm plate as a guide, trim to a perfect circle. Carefully lift onto a baking tray lined with baking parchment. (Re-roll the trimmings to make smaller biscuits, if you like.)

4 Using a large knife, score the dough into 8 sections, without cutting all the way through, then lightly press 2 dimples on the edge of each wedge with your thumb. Cover loosely and chill for at least an hour to firm up.

5 Preheat the oven to 160°C/Gas 2½. Remove the shortbread from the fridge and place in the oven. Bake for 20–30 minutes until firm and pale golden in colour. Leave on the baking tray for a minute then, using a palette knife, lift onto a wire rack to cool. Sprinkle with caster sugar while still warm.

6 Once cooled, break the shortbread round along the indentations into wedges and store in an airtight tin until ready to serve.

There's nothing quite like buttery homemade shortbread, especially at Christmas. It can also form the basis for a speedy dessert: lay the shortbread round on a plate and top each marked portion with a spoonful of crème fraîche, the finely grated zest of a clementine and a peeled clementine half or segments.

The addition of dried cranberries makes these mince pies extra special. You can use a jar of luxury mincemeat, but better to make it yourself. For convenience, prepare the pies well ahead and freeze unbaked for up to a month, then just glaze and pop straight into the oven when you want to eat them, allowing an extra 5–10 minutes.

CRANBERRY MINCE PIES

MAKES 24

Pastry:

250g plain flour, plus extra to dust

25g icing sugar

125g chilled unsalted butter, diced

finely grated zest of 1 orange

1 medium egg, lightly beaten

1–3 tsp ice-cold water (if needed)

Filling:

400g jar good-quality mincemeat
   (or use home-made, see below)

150g dried cranberries

To finish:

1 egg yolk, beaten with 1 tsp water
   (eggwash), to glaze

icing sugar or caster sugar, to dust

1 For the pastry, put the flour, icing sugar, butter and orange zest into a food processor and whiz to fine crumbs. With the motor running, add the egg and whiz for a few seconds until the mixture forms clumps and you can press it together into a ball. (If necessary, add 1–3 tsp ice-cold water to bring the dough together.)

2 Turn onto a very lightly floured surface and knead briefly until smooth. Wrap in cling film and chill for at least 30 minutes, or until firm. (The pastry can be made up to 3 days ahead or frozen for up to a month.)

3 For the filling, turn the mincemeat into a bowl and stir in the dried cranberries. Roll out the pastry on a lightly floured surface to the thickness of a £1 coin. Using an 8cm fluted cutter, cut out 24 rounds and use to line two 12-hole non-stick mince pie tins.

4 Re-roll the trimmings to the same thickness and stamp out 24 stars or Christmas trees, with an appropriate cutter, for the tops. Put a dessertspoonful (2 tsp) filling into each pastry case, then press the tops in position. Chill for at least 20 minutes. Meanwhile, preheat the oven to 180°C/Gas 4.

5 Brush the tops with the eggwash, then bake the mince pies for 15–20 minutes until the pastry is golden and crisp. Let cool for a few minutes before removing from the tins and transferring to a wire rack to cool. Store an airtight container for up to 1 week. Warm slightly before serving, with a dusting of sugar.

MINCEMEAT

Peel and grate a large dessert apple into a big bowl. Add the grated zest and juice of 1 lemon and 1 orange, then 110g suet, 240g raisins, 110g diced dried apricots, 175g soft dark brown sugar, 50g flaked almonds, 1½ tsp ground allspice, 1 tsp ground cinnamon, ¾ tsp ground nutmeg, 50ml brandy and 50ml dark rum. Stir well, then cover and chill for 30 minutes. If not using immediately, transfer to clean sterilised jars and store in the fridge. The mincemeat improves the longer you let it mature, but should be used within 6 months. MAKES ABOUT 1.25KG (ENOUGH FOR 3 BATCHES OF MINCE PIES)

CINNAMON AND ALMOND DRIZZLE CAKE

SERVES 8

250g lightly salted butter

groundnut or sunflower oil, to oil

50g plain flour, plus 1–2 tbsp to dust

2 tsp ground cinnamon

175g golden caster sugar

250g finely ground almonds

100g golden syrup

6 large egg whites

Icing (optional):

150g icing sugar

1 tbsp lime or lemon juice

2 tbsp double cream

To finish (optional):

silver balls or other edible festive
    decorations

icing sugar, to dust

1 Melt the butter in a heavy-based saucepan over a low heat. Increase the temperature and cook the butter until it starts to turn brown. Watch carefully as you don't want to let it burn, which can happen quickly. Immediately take off the heat and let it stand for a few minutes to allow the milk solids to settle. Slowly pour off the fat into a bowl, leaving the solids behind; discard these. Let the butter cool to room temperature.

2 Preheat the oven to 160°C/Gas 2½. Oil a 23cm wide bundt tin or other ring-shaped cake tin (2–2.5 litre capacity) and lightly dust the base and sides with a little flour. Sift the flour and cinnamon into a large bowl and stir in the sugar and ground almonds.

3 Beat the golden syrup and egg whites together in another bowl, using an electric whisk, until light and fluffy, about 1–2 minutes. Fold the cooled butter into the dry mixture, followed by the whisked egg whites.

4 Spoon the mixture evenly into the prepared tin and bake for 40–50 minutes, or until a skewer inserted into the centre of the cake comes out clean. Leave to cool in the tin on a wire rack.

5 To unmould, gently press the cake away from the sides of the tin with your fingertips and then invert onto a large plate or cake stand.

6 For the icing, if required, mix the ingredients together in a bowl until smooth, then spoon on top of the cake, letting it drizzle down the sides attractively. Finish, if you wish, with silver balls or other decorations. Cut into slices to serve. If the cake is simply dusted with icing sugar, you might like to serve it with vanilla ice cream or cream.

This is based on my recipe for financier, a French almondy sponge. Made with browned butter to give the sponge an additional rich, nutty taste, this version is lovely and moist. The sweet icing is optional; you may prefer a simple dusting of icing sugar instead.

WHITE CHOCOLATE BISCOTTI
WITH PISTACHIOS
AND DRIED CRANBERRIES

MAKES ABOUT 60

225g plain flour, plus extra to dust

1 tsp ground mixed spice

1 tsp baking powder

pinch of fine sea salt

170g golden caster sugar

2 medium eggs

1 tsp vanilla extract

50g good-quality white chocolate, chopped into small pieces

50g shelled unsalted pistachio nuts

50g dried cranberries

1 medium egg white, to glaze

1 Preheat the oven to 170°C/Gas 3. Line a large baking sheet with a silicone liner. Sift the flour, mixed spice, baking powder and salt into a large bowl. Stir in the sugar and make a well in the centre.

2 In another bowl, beat the eggs with the vanilla extract. Pour into the well in the dry ingredients and mix with a spatula, then use your hands to press the dough together to form a ball. It may seem too dry at first, but persevere and it will come together. Knead in the chopped chocolate, pistachios and dried cranberries.

3 Turn the dough out onto a lightly floured surface and divide into 4 equal pieces. Roll each portion into a long log, about 2–3cm in diameter, then lift onto the lined baking sheet, spacing the logs well apart.

4 Lightly whisk the egg white until just frothy and brush over the top of the dough. Bake for 20 minutes until risen and firm, but still pale. Set the biscotti logs aside to cool for about 10–15 minutes and lower the oven setting to 120°C/Gas ½.

5 Using a serrated knife, cut the logs into 1cm thick slices on the diagonal. Lay the slices on the baking sheet and bake for 10 minutes. Turn them over and bake for another 10 minutes until dry and lightly golden.

6 Transfer to a wire rack and leave to cool completely. Store in an airtight container until ready to serve, or pack in sealable gift bags.

These biscotti make a delightful food gift at Christmas, but you need to pack them in airtight containers to keep them crunchy. Enjoy with a strong coffee or try them dipped in Vin Santo for a light dessert.

MINT CHOCOLATE TRUFFLES

MAKES 80–90

250ml double cream

250ml single cream

small bunch of mint

500g good-quality dark chocolate
(about 70% cocoa solids)

130g butter, diced

130g clear honey

Coating:

one or more of the following: cocoa
powder, crushed chocolate flake bars,
crushed amaretti biscuits, finely
chopped pistachio nuts or almonds

1 Pour both creams into a medium saucepan. Lightly bash the mint sprigs with a wooden spoon to release their fragrance and add them to the pan. Heat very gently for 5–6 minutes to infuse the cream with the mint.

2 Meanwhile, break up the chocolate and place in a heatproof bowl with the diced butter and honey.

3 Strain the hot cream through a sieve onto the chocolate, butter and honey, stirring as you do so; discard the mint sprigs. Continue to stir until the chocolate has melted and the mixture is smooth.

4 Pour the mixture into a wide, shallow dish, cover and chill in the fridge for an hour, or until firm.

5 Scatter your chosen coating(s) on separate plates. Take the truffle mix from the fridge and, using a teaspoon, scoop out a portion and shape into a sphere by quickly rolling it in your hands. (Do this speedily to avoid the truffle melting with the warmth of your hands.) Toss the truffle in your preferred coating and arrange on a plate. Repeat with the rest.

6 Place the truffles in a shallow plastic container, seal and refrigerate until firm and ready to serve. Eat within 3–4 days.

One of my golden rules for Christmas is to delegate. At home, I'm raising my own little brigade of sous chefs, who are always willing to help with any recipe that involves chocolate and the possibility of licking the spoon – this one certainly appeals. Instead of mint, you might like to flavour the chocolate truffles with a splash of brandy, or grated orange zest and a little Grand Marnier, or even fresh chilli to give a surprising but delicious kick.

INDEX